HORIZON

MAY, 1977 • VOLUME XIX, NUMBER 3

HORIZON

MAY, 1977 • VOLUME XIX, NUMBER 3

HORIZON is published six times a year by American Heritage Publishing Co., Inc. Editorial and executive offices: 10 Rockefeller Plaza, New York, N.Y. 10020. Treasurer and Secretary: Anthony J. Sansiveri. All correspondence about subscriptions should be addressed to: HORIZON Subscription Office, 381 West Center St., Marion, Ohio 43302.

Single copies: $5.00. Subscriptions: $21.00 per year in the U.S.; Canada and elsewhere: $23.00.
Hard-cover edition: Single copies: $7.50. Subscriptions: $27.00 per year in the U.S.; Canada and elsewhere: $29.00.

Cumulative indexes for Volumes I–V, VI–X, and XI–XV are available at $7.50. HORIZON is also indexed in the *Readers' Guide to Periodical Literature*. The editors welcome contributions but can assume no responsibility for unsolicited material. Title registered U.S. Patent Office. Second-class postage paid at New York, N.Y., and at additional mailing offices.

A New Direction

With this issue we begin a new chapter in HORIZON's history.

Since its beginning in 1958, HORIZON has been a magazine devoted to the understanding of culture, especially to the insights provided by history, archaeology, and the artistic masterpieces of the past. In the first issue of HORIZON, the editors set forth a definition of culture as "both achievement and dream, a work of the hands and a movement of the spirit, . . . art and ideas, past and present, taken in sum as a guide to life . . . a birthright which we all inherit."

This sense of our cultural heritage is the foundation on which we build, but from now on we will concern ourselves primarily with the contemporary world.

The photographs and the table of contents opposite give an indication of the scope and approach of this transitional issue.

Our particular province is urban life—in all its diversity and complexity, including the life of the suburbs and exurbs that depend on the cities for much of their vitality.

We will, as in the past, be concerned with the arts, but the emphasis will be on the current scene and on all the arts—popular and classical, performing as well as visual.

We will be looking at urban life through the eyes of artists, movie makers, television directors, playwrights, novelists, and sociologists. We will be reporting on the ways in which architecture and urban planning shape our environment.

We will examine the intellectual and social trends generated in the great metropolitan centers—new trends in education, the political and moral questions that affect urban and suburban families, and the changes that science brings in our lives. Not forgetting the pleasures of food and drink, and changes in style and fashion.

We will continue in our concern for history, especially those events of the past and those areas of the world that suddenly take on current meaning. And we will regularly make room for the splendors of the past —the great works of art, the archaeological finds, the historical places revisited—that constitute our cultural heritage.

We will endeavor to be in the mainstream of contemporary thought and artistic activity and to inform educated and active Americans about themselves and their world.

Contents

At a Glance

COVER: A detail of *The Virgin*, a painting by Andrew Wyeth
featured in an article beginning on page 24.

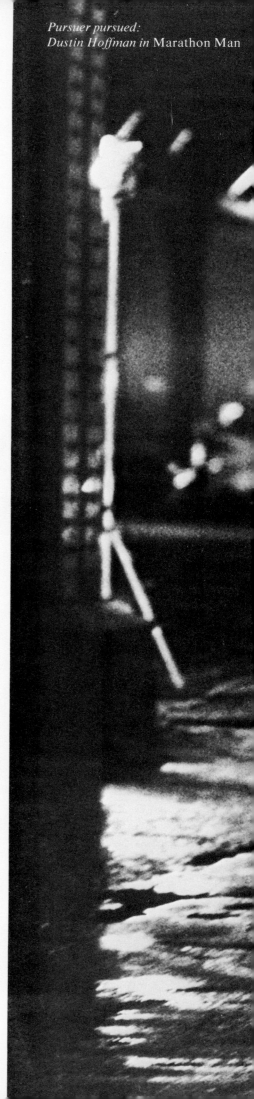

Those Mean and Dirty Streets

The city in recent films is a
place of violence, squalor, degradation, and
boredom, leaving many an urban
moviegoer bewildered about where he lives

The pavement vents clouds of steam, which turn the city scene into a hellish murk. A taxicab moves slowly through, like a yellow fish in a heavy sea. Times Square's cheerful, tacky neon is blurred and drained of life. And the sallow face of Robert De Niro takes in everything and gets it wrong. The walls of his rented room are shiny, the windows are padlocked, there are candy wrappers on the floor, vitamin bottles and Wonder Bread on the shelf.

This is how the movie *Taxi Driver* sees the city of New York. In a movie of fifteen years ago the cabs would have been clean, shined up, and slightly out of focus: part of the background against which some quirky romance—*Breakfast at Tiffany's*, for instance—was played out. Ten years before that Gene Kelly would have climbed out dancing, as the cabbie and passers-by beamed.

Like unsecured cargo on a pitching deck, American films ride our shifting notions of the urban reality always a little out of phase and harder than the lurches themselves. Our cities never were playgrounds, even when the movies made them seem so. When movie crews scrubbed and polished the taxis and took care that the extras on the park bench wore clean shirts, the city was made to look more glamorous than it was. Today, when cameras focus on the nerve-racked faces in *Taxi Driver*, on the victims and perpetrators of the bank holdup in *Dog Day Afternoon*, or on the drifters in *Midnight Cowboy*, they make city life seem more terrible than it is. Despite its troubles, the American city still supports life and along with it a whole assortment of hopes, virtues, and pleasures that the current movies manage to ignore.

Of course both the beautiful and terrible things are always there, and in quantity. But the movie camera, unless it is in the hands of a master (such as Jean Renoir or François Truffaut), has no peripheral vision. It tends to concentrate all the resources of film-making—lighting, timing, costumes, the prop man who comes variously to sweep up cigarette butts or to spread them—for particular effects. Movies are rarely capable of metaphors. Or rather the metaphors become so overwhelming that they take over. On a hot day we say: "It's an oven outside"; the movie shows such crimson faces, so much sweat, and heat haze so dense that the oven becomes almost literal. Newspaper editorials announce that cities are dying, and the writers and readers go cheerfully off to lunch. Movies stick us with urban graveyards.

Over the years when American optimism frayed, the movies not only caught up with the swing but swung

By RICHARD EDER

Whore and cabbie: Jodie Foster and Robert De Niro in Taxi Driver

Subway avenger: Charles Bronson in Death Wish

Embittered idealist: Bill Holden in Network

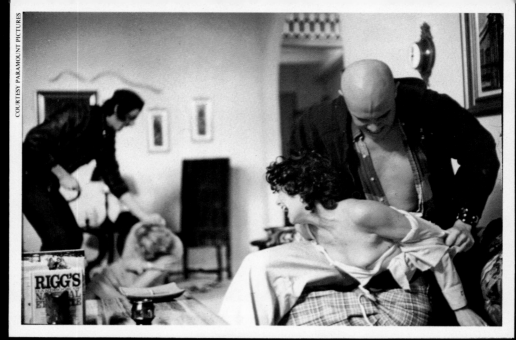

Rape and battery in Death Wish

We are in a dark cave, the figures in it are all menacing and, to one degree or other, evil.

harder. At the same time they dealt more and more with urban subjects and settings. How many films about small-town or country life are made anymore? In the thirties and forties they came out regularly; comedies, romances, even satires, were set as often in the small towns as in the cities.

Nowadays we get an occasional film about murderousness in the wide open spaces: the vindictive small-towners of *Easy Rider* who shoot down the wandering young motorcyclists; the bloody, bank-robbing swing around the American hinterland of *Bonnie and Clyde*; the murderous young pair in *Badlands* who set up as outlaws and kill anyone they come across. But for the most part country themes are in the hands of the Walt Disney people, who turn them out full of instant charm. Or they are found in the newer genre of southern red-dirt pictures such as *Macon County Line* and its successors. Westerns are all but gone, except for parodies or ponderous

memorials like John Wayne's geriatric *Shootist*. The cowboys have put on policemen's uniforms, live messily in the city, and are a lot meaner.

. . .

In nineteenth-century America conquering the world meant going west. In the twentieth century, when Hollywood got started, it came to mean going to the city. The city as hope: it may seem a curiosity now. Certainly it would to anyone going to the movies these past years. When *My Sister Eileen* was made twenty years ago, it was taken for granted that two pretty sisters could come to New York from Columbus, Ohio, and get into only minor trouble. Nobody expected them to be robbed, raped, polluted, or driven to hang out in singles bars.

Of course the city was treated in other ways as well. There were gangster films and films that took some real view of urban desolation and heartlessness. Even in Frank Capra's social fantasies,

when Mr. Deeds went to town or Mr. Smith went to Washington, they encountered plenty of chicanery. Yet the hopefulness was there. For that matter, the make-it-big myth still hasn't disappeared from the movies—it never will as long as there are cities—but it has taken twisted forms. For example, Jon Voight in *Midnight Cowboy*: slicked up in his best hick suit, he rides the bus all the way to New York with visions in his head. But the visions are of the rich women he will pick up and sleep with for money.

A good many older Hollywood movies took the city for granted, used it exclusively as a background for whatever story they were telling. This taking for granted was itself a kind of attitude about the city, an expectation, at least, that the streets and sidewalks would yield no disagreeable surprises. In fact, the studio-built city backgrounds of the 1930's musicals were abstractions. In *Top Hat* Fred Astaire and Ginger Rogers moved around in a haze of assurance, but it was almost all interiors; and when they did go out into a park and got rained upon, they didn't get wet. "Isn't This a Lovely Day to Be Caught in the Rain" was sung and danced in the shelter of a gazebo.

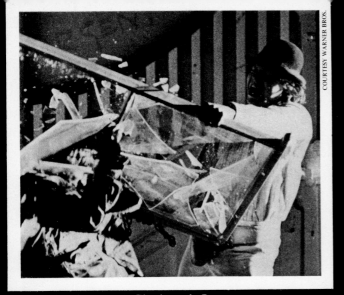

Casual violence in A Clockwork Orange

Casual murderer (Sir Laurence Olivier) in Marathon Man

By the late forties and early fifties, when Gene Kelly went out in the rain, it soaked him. *On the Town, Singin' in the Rain*, and any number of other films put the actors on more real-looking streets —sometimes on actual streets. At the same time they took everybody else off the streets and filled them with extras. The cities acquired identities—earlier, films had shown them in a generalized way without naming them—but the life in them was made up.

They served as lively settings. Their movement and elegance was pointed up by the directors and cameramen. They provided something big and exciting for the main characters to show themselves against. One of the characteristic scenes in those films was the throwing-your-self-upon-the-city scene. It was like jumping into the surf. Kelly and Frank Sinatra would dance around policemen, circle old ladies, take an apple from a fruit stand. Nobody would pull a knife. The city loved them.

In *Breakfast at Tiffany's*—a blend of mechanical poignance and calculated charm—there was a Wonderful Immersion. Audrey Hepburn and George Peppard flung themselves around town; the camera aimed upward, and we saw a lot of gleaming buildings and no trash. They did cute things at the Public Library and Tiffany's, and finally shoplifted two animal masks at Woolworth's and danced home in them. The weather was chosen for clarity: those twenty-four blue days New York gets each year that make it look magnificent. It rained now and then, for mood and contrast, but you never had the true gray stickiness. The city was treated as an adventure; hearts were broken but not heads. People from next-door were invited in, and when the doors shut, there was only one lock on them.

A Thousand Clowns, a much better movie made in 1965, reflected some of the same. Jason Robards played a man who gave up a career to lead a rambling life with his comically serious young nephew. They wandered around junk yards and construction sites, flew kites in Central Park, visited the piers to wave at departing passengers. They were bohemians—the word has since lost all meaning—fighting the gray purpose-fulness of the city. But that's all the city was being attacked for. It was a sharp-nosed and interfering aunt, not a drug-crazed and dangerous nephew. It was without menace and full of liberat-

ing things to do. Even the slums were picturesque. And Robards was an eccentric. It takes a lot of stability to produce eccentrics, and nowadays movies don't feature them. They have desperate people, madmen, neurotics; but not eccentrics.

Even films about crime and corruption in the city treated those themes in a far different way than they are treated nowadays. They were specific diseases in an organism of some health and beauty rather than a general declaration of epidemic and quarantine.

On the Waterfront, of 1954, was about the murderous control exercised by union bosses over the lives of longshore-men. The bosses were despots, the waterfront workers passive and resigned. But the movie set up a struggle: a young longshoreman, Marlon Brando, who gradually turned against the bosses; his idealistic girl friend, Eva Marie Saint; and a priest, Karl Malden. These three fought and, eventually, won.

The theme that the ordinary man, with bravery and persistence, can defeat evil makes *Waterfront* very different from the dead visions of *Network* and *Marathon Man*. In the first, cynical television executives, ignoring the scruples

7

Button-down reveler: Robert Redford in Barefoot in the Park *(1967)*

Wacky party girl: Audrey Hepburn in Breakfast at Tiffany's *(1961)*

of the single fair man among them, decide to keep using a newscaster who has gone mad on the air when it turns out that the public likes to hear him rant. The television audience is as degraded as the broadcasters. In the second, an innocent young man pursued by mysterious undercover agents can find no help anywhere except, briefly, from a Spanish-American street gang. In the end he saves himself by killing as savagely as his pursuers.

Waterfront has heroes as well as villains. And there is something else, too. The director and cameraman are able to find considerable beauty in the unpromising setting of a city waterfront. Above the dingy row-apartments there is the poetry of the roof tops. Children play there; adults go to talk or be alone or raise pigeons. There is the little strip of a waterfront park, grimy, fenced, but with a wonderful misty view of escape: Manhattan and the Hudson River. There are the lovely faces of Brando and Saint. These are not just decorations. They establish a value, a sense of the good. We are given a notion of order, something to hold on to, a lantern.

Over the last dozen years movies have tended to throw the lantern away. We

are in a dark cave, the figures in it are all menacing and, to one degree or other, evil. There are no heroes. Ranged against the wicked are either victims—Dustin Hoffman as the *Marathon Man*, William Holden as the decent television executive in *Network*—or brutes, such as Gene Hackman, the crude but persistent cop in *The French Connection*.

As for the city—which is these movies' image for humanity in general—it is no longer simply a place where bad things happen. It is bad in itself.

Curiously, in *The French Connection*, for all its ferocious violence, some restraint is exercised in the treatment of New York. There is evil in the streets, but the streets look pretty good. Manhattan's East Side has its style; a man in a restaurant (true, he is a bad man) is eating good food with pleasure; the fruit in a fruit stand looks fresh and sweet; and the brickwork of Harlem, lit by an early-morning sun, has beauty. The camera looks at things as if it liked them. The effect is to hint that contamination, though widespread, is not quite all-pervasive.

But a great many other movies find nothing at all to salvage from our cities. In *Network* we are made to feel con-

tempt not only for the sharks in the television studios but also for the populace at large. The camera looks at the city and finds only the stupid and credulous faces that bob along in it. When the mad telecaster tells people to open their windows and shout, we see whole buildings turn into rows of shouting heads. (One thing New Yorkers won't do is do anything all together at the same time.)

In *Marathon Man* the workings of the secret organization that is after Dustin Hoffman are complemented by the murderous irascibility of some people in the "ordinary" street scenes and the equally murderous indifference of others. Not a single car stops for Hoffman as he flees on foot across the Queensboro Bridge. Even in *King Kong* the city crowds are hysterical and greedy.

The photography and music of *Taxi Driver* deliberately make the city ugly, sticky, sinister. Each person is isolated, shut in by fear of others, and the only communication is the temporary exchange of delusions. The isolation is most extreme in the case of Robert De Niro. When he and Cybill Shepherd are together, it is not two people touching but fragile and mismatched fantasies.

When the movie camera turns away

Lovable tough and his girl: Marlon Brando and Eva Marie Saint in On the Waterfront *(1954)*

Debonair dropout: Jason Robards in A Thousand Clowns *(1965)*

It takes a lot of stability to produce eccentrics, and nowadays movies don't feature them.

from the violent streets and focuses on the middle and upper classes, desperation and isolation are still the rule, but in more stylish surroundings. *Such Good Friends* is a story of self-involved, neurotic style-setters out of touch with reality. It is a funny and acute movie—and terribly bleak. In its city of sophisticates everyone talks, but vocal as they are, nobody says anything. And if somebody does manage to cry "Help"—Dyan Cannon does, eventually, when her husband dies—nobody listens.

The Prisoner of Second Avenue is a satirical catalogue of miseries conveyed in wisecracks that flow like tears. Jack Lemmon and Anne Bancroft have the good life; that is, their expensive walls crack, their expensive toilet leaks, their expensive terrace stinks from the uncollected garbage below, they are burgled, he is fired. They cannot dismount from their tension; they cling to each other and are totally isolated. There is nothing they belong to: society, except as the sum of laws, jobs, places to go, and things to buy, no longer exists.

Both these pictures, not incidentally, were shot in the summer, when New York's light is at its ugliest. The streets are steamy, there are no shadows,

and Central Park looks worm-eaten.

Another group of films sees the life of urban humanity as closer to madness than misery. In their extremes of wild humor and savagery they are oddly more human than many of the pictures mentioned so far. *Little Murders* is one of these. In it the violence of Manhattan is carried to a demented extreme. People are continually being shot down in the street, a housewife comes home with a bullet hole in her shopping bag, and the police have become shaky neurotics. Elliot Gould drifts apathetically through the mess until his wife is shot dead as he embraces her. Then he joins the ranks of the snipers and is last seen blazing away—happily—from an upper-story window.

Then there is a masterpiece, *A Clockwork Orange*, which was directed by Stanley Kubrick. It is a vision of the city of the future. Slums have been replaced by lavishly gadgeted and sterile apartments, but they are inhabited by

the same old slum dwellers. Regulated abundance is the answer to every human need except the need to be human. Violence, divorced from any material cause, becomes something between a drug and a religion.

Kubrick conducts us through the violence; he never turns it upon us. He uses slow motion, balletlike movements, and distance. The mass rape of a girl is shocking but abstract, because the figures are in long-shot and we never see their faces. Above all, he shows us the violent act without the violent result. When Malcolm MacDowell smashes a stone sculpture down on a woman, we see the act of murder but not the wounds of the victim. No other film manages to show so movingly the horror of violence while avoiding complicity in it.

• • •

American movies have always been good at the single impact, whether it is humor, excitement, delight, or despair. They have been far weaker than Euro-

9

Loser who fights back: Jack Lemmon in
The Prisoner of Second Avenue

*Rare winners: Sylvester Stallone
and Talia Shire in* Rocky

**What most American films don't see is how things heal
in cities; they show only how the wounds are made.**

---

pean films in dealing with the complexities of social relationships. They give us pieces of the city—pieces, not slices—as they give us pieces of life.

At their best, the movies have always provided some particular set of truths about the city. (They have ignored a great deal, too: work, the politics and ordinary transactions of city existence, and—with brilliant exceptions such as *The Little Fugitive*—children.) The glossy, big-city excitement of the 1950's musicals is a very real part of New York. But those films left out the grittiness, the oppression, the weariness and ruin of lives. Today the movies tend to leave out the vitality, the beauty, and the occasional joyfulness that persist in spurting up among all the ugliness and civic incompetence that our cities give us.

The typical movie of today isolates some one perception and matches everything to it. Does casual sex leave a bad aftertaste? Can it be emotionally destructive? The recent movie *Welcome to*

L.A. seizes the idea tenaciously. An attempt to show spiritual death in the fat neighborhoods of Los Angeles—but in the end a sort of fashion layout for a product named despair—the movie makes every part of the sexual encounter joyless. Movies, like Calvinist preachers, make the hangover conterminous with the drinking.

In life, danger simply makes a city dangerous. It does other things; too—it tires people—but it doesn't really contaminate all of life. Some people cannot tolerate danger, but anyone who has been in Belfast knows how much wit, grace, and desire to make the best of things remain among the horrors.

Films about the city-as-terror show little or nothing of this. They do not show the indeterminacy of situations and people. One of those cars on the Queensboro Bridge would have stopped for Dustin Hoffman. The movies do not see the need of people for warmth in the harshest circumstances, or their inge-

nuity in finding it, in creating it. They don't watch New Yorkers—strangers—getting off a bus and painstakingly holding the door open for one another. The movies don't go for a container of coffee four times at the same hole-in-the-wall lunch counter and see how their anonymity is dissolved by the counterman.

A movie that does some of these things, like *Rocky*, seems a revelation. The story of a goodhearted incompetent boxer who becomes a goodhearted successful one, *Rocky* is full of people from the slums of Philadelphia who still feel for one another and respect themselves. Most notable is Rocky himself, a tough but sensitive guy who works as a Mafia bagman until he gets his big chance—and then makes the best of it.

What most current American films don't see is how things heal in cities and in people; they show only how the wounds are made. The movies give us the city as an ash heap because it looks like one; they don't see that it is a banked fire that is constantly reviving in the most unexpected places. ☐

A one-time foreign correspondent, Richard Eder currently writes about film and theatre for the New York Times.

A QUARTET OF SPECTACULARS

The hottest show in town these days is likely to be playing in the halls of an art museum. Earlier this year, Andrew Wyeth's paintings and drawings were a hit at Manhattan's Metropolitan Museum of Art, and three traveling shows—treasures from Tutankhamun's tomb, "Calder's Universe," and a retrospective of Robert Rauschenberg's work—are drawing thousands across the country.

Each of the shows delivers handsomely what the critic Herbert Read once said people seek in all art: "a certain personal element . . . a unique and private vision of the world." Tutankhamun's artists envisioned eternity and made ritual objects like the graceful goddess Selket (top, left) to live forever. Rauschenberg (top, right), seeking to close the gap between art and life, uses whatever means are at hand. Alexander Calder, that giant of American art, had a vision of cosmic proportions, and his work ranged from the monumental to the playful (above, left) with astounding ease. Wyeth, whose painting of *The Virgin* (above, right) surprised many who think of him as a cool technician, characterizes his art as a continual challenge to combine "my absolutely mad freedom and excitement with truth."

American museumgoers seem happy to entertain a variety of truths as long as a "private vision," nourishing and replenishing the spirit, can be found. On the following pages, HORIZON goes beyond the exhibitions to present the museum stars of 1977.

King Tut Rises Again

One morning's line at the National Gallery

On a cold day in January, when, by President-elect Carter's own command, the nation was cutting back its ceremonial acclaim for the fifty-two-year-old peanut farmer from Georgia, a Washington cab driver was asked why he was so anxious to see the King Tut exhibition at the National Gallery. "They did all that for a nineteen-year-old kid," he said, shaking his head in wonderment. For other spectators there was the thrill of seeing what had once been laid to rest for eternity, as well as the pleasure of delving into ancient history. The result was endless crowds averaging almost seven thousand people a day.

In 1924 Tutankhamun's mummy, encased in three coffins, was raised from the dark solitude of his tomb (below, left), under the watchful eyes of Howard Carter, a British Egyptologist. "The greatest archaeological discovery of all time," as one contemporary newspaper put it, touched off a mania for all things Egyptian—a rage that lasted well into the thirties. Fashionable women in Europe and America sported scarab pendants and heavy jeweled collars; Pharaoh's chairs turned up in the most stylish modern living rooms; movie palaces installed friezes of Egyptian figures in profile; bronze inkwells had stoppers that were replicas of Tutankhamun's head.

Now a new King Tut craze is upon us, coming in the wake of an extraordinary exhibition, "Treasures of Tutankhamun," currently at the Field Museum of Natural History in Chicago, and scheduled to proceed later this year and next to New Orleans, Los Angeles, Seattle, and New York. A triumph of showmanship, the exhibition re-creates the excitement of the original discovery and the "sense of vanished but haunting forces" that Carter said he felt in the tomb. Visitors to the exhibition go through darkened chambers where dramatically lit Lucite cases display gold jewelry inlaid with gemstones and polychrome glass, alabaster vases and statues, intricately carved wooden chests, model boats and gaming boards, miniature gold effigies of goddesses, and portraits of the young Pharaoh himself. Each piece is a masterpiece of its kind, and on the walls are enlarged photographs taken during the excavation that show exactly where everything was found.

Taking quick advantage of the mounting interest in Tutankhamun, the museums themselves are selling reproductions of items in the show. Springmaid has launched its "Along the Nile" collection of bed and bath linens (below), and King Tut dinner plates and T-shirts are turning up in department stores. All the hoopla may not be the afterlife the ancient Egyptians intended for their Pharaoh, but it is, in its way, a kind of immortality.

Hoisting the coffins of Tutankhamun, 1924

The winged figure of Isis is the motif for Springmaid's sheets and quilt.

13

The Three Faces of Tut

Among the most striking pieces in the show, these portraits of Tutankhamun, made of translucent alabaster (right), a single piece of carved wood (opposite), and solid gold, beaten and burnished (below), attest to the extraordinary skill of the artists who fashioned them some 3,300 years ago. A handsome young man, Tutankhamun had been Pharaoh for less than ten years when he died, at the age of nineteen, in 1325 B.C. His predecessor, and probably his father, was the iconoclastic Akhenaten, who banned polytheism and worshiped a single deity, Aten, in a new capital city at Amarna. Tutankhamun and his regents reversed these changes, reviving the worship of the old gods and restoring the capital to Thebes. Little is known of Tutankhamun's personal life: he was married to the daughter of Akhenaten and Nefertiti, he enjoyed hunting ostriches, and he may once have fought in battle. A slight crack on his skull has led to the suspicion that he may have been assassinated. Certainly his death came suddenly, for his tomb was hastily constructed and unusually small. But who would have wanted to do him in, or why, remains a mystery.

This small alabaster portrait was once the stopper for a compartment of a chest containing the dead Pharaoh's viscera; the wood effigy opposite was designed to do chores that the king would rather skip; and the mask below, the most famous image of King Tut, was placed over the head and shoulders of his mummy.

Rauschenberg: The World Is a Painting

COLLECTION OF MR. AND MRS. SIDNEY SINGER — COURTESY LEO CASTELLI GALLERY

Enter the picture: *Free-swinging doors distinguish Rauschenberg's* Rodeo Palace (Spread), *completed last year.*

Robert Rauschenberg, the sixties' King of Pop and Merlin of Happenings, is back, this time as the subject of a major retrospective now drawing crowds at the Museum of Modern Art in New York. The show, which will travel to San Francisco, Buffalo, and Chicago, consists of some 160 works—paintings, drawings, silk-screen prints, sculptures, and constructions the artist calls "combines"—that joyfully express Rauschenberg's antiformalism and, occasionally, a kind of ethereal beauty.

One of the latest pieces in the exhibit, *Rodeo Palace (Spread)*, is almost an autobiographical retrospective in itself. The piece commemorates the Fort Worth rodeo, and its rich melee of images—including a pail, a Venus flytrap, a horse, and an oil derrick—reflects what Rauschenberg termed the "rural opulence" of his home state of Texas. One of the painting's three doors opens onto mattress ticking reminiscent of an earlier

piece, *Bed* (his own quilt, sheet, and pillow mounted and painted), that enraged critics in 1955.

In his other combines, as in *Rodeo*, Rauschenberg allows the shape, texture, and symbolism of such objects as packing crates, newspapers, a stuffed bird, or a broken umbrella to determine the nature of the work. Since the sixties he has sought to widen his range of materials and techniques by studying lithography in this country and papermaking and silk dyeing in France and India. The results can be seen in his two recent series *Hoarfrost* and *Jammers*, in which silk and gauzy materials, some printed with images, ripple with every movement of air, thus literally incorporating the room's atmosphere into the art. Ever seeking to close the gap between art and life, Rauschenberg continues to demonstrate his dictum: "There is no reason not to consider the world one gigantic painting."

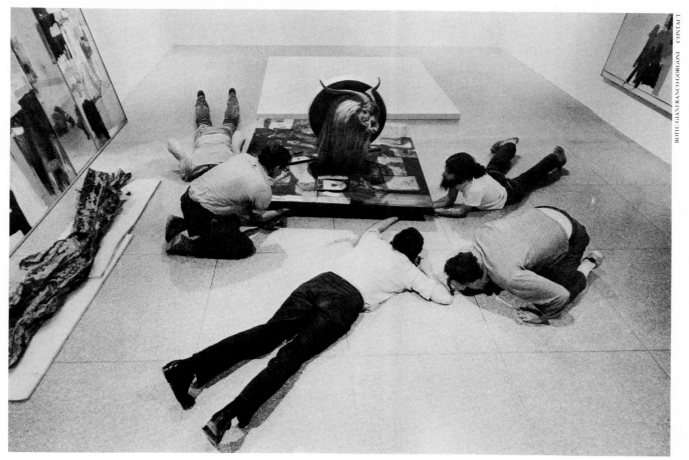

Putting it together: *Before his traveling show opened in Washington, the artist (above in foreground) installed* Monogram, *a tire-girdled goat, and (below)* Sor Agua, *a bathtub with crushed metal hanging overhead.*

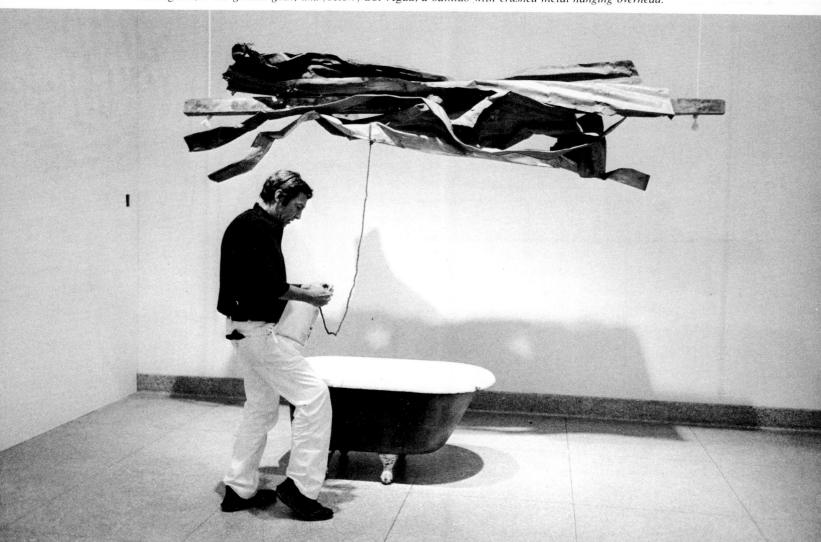

HERBERT MIGDOLL

Rauschenberg on stage: *the set for* Minutiae, *first performed by the Merce Cunningham dance troupe, 1954*

BOTH: PETER MOORE

Costumes: *for Rauschenberg, a pail . . .*   *for dancer, a cage with doves*

DAVID WHARTON

A new medium: *editing a video-taped dance performance in Fort Worth*

Acting, Directing, Designing

"Theatre remains one of the most demanding and purest forms of art," Rauschenberg once said. "There is no separation of life and work. The individual is the medium." Throughout the fifties and sixties he worked on costumes, lighting, sets, and choreography for performances with John Cage, the avant-garde composer, and Merce Cunningham, the dancer and choreographer. In *Pelican*, directed by Rauschenberg in 1963, the artist himself appeared, wearing roller skates and a parachute. Often live animals participated; in *Spring Training* thirty turtles carrying tiny flashlights on their backs ambled across the stage. The form and even sometimes the cast of the exuberant productions changed constantly, for Rauschenberg was more concerned with the process of people reacting to one another and their environment than in a final product.

After a long respite from theatrical concerns, Rauschenberg again designed sets, costumes, and lighting for a Cunningham piece, *Travelogue*, which won acclaim on Broadway earlier this year. Charting yet another course for his art, Rauschenberg recently worked in his native Texas editing and altering the color of a video tape of a dance performance for public television.

Merce Cunningham performs in the new Rauschenberg-designed Travelogue

Calder: He Gave Pleasure

KAREN SKELTON

Children and adults surround Calder's stabile The Crab. *Kids love Calder; he once said, "My fan mail is enormous — everybody is under six."*

When Alexander Calder died last November at the age of seventy-eight, one of the largest retrospectives of his work had just opened at New York's Whitney Museum, an exhibition that recently left Atlanta and will travel to Minneapolis this summer and to Dallas in the fall. No memorial to the charming Calder, the most popular American sculptor of the century, could be more fitting than this vivacious show with its twirling and dipping mobiles and its monumental stabiles looking like dinosaurs in a Museum of Fanciful History.

For all its exuberant simplicity, Calder's art represents a complex fusion of many elements. In one sense his giant stabiles (one at the Massachusetts Institute of Technology is forty feet high and weighs twenty-five tons) are part of a family tradition of heroic sculpture. His grandfather made the thirty-

seven-foot-tall statue of William Penn atop Philadelphia's City Hall, and his father sculpted George Washington for the arch at the foot of Manhattan's Fifth Avenue.

Seen in another light, Calder's ingenious forms recall the work of Yankee tinkerers. As a little boy he had a studio in the basement, and among his earliest extant works are a tiny saddle and hat he fashioned for his sister's dolls when he was nine. His interest in devising curiosities with wire and pliers never abated, and his first distinctive sculpture was a wire portrait of the jazz singer Josephine Baker made in 1926. Throughout his life he continued to twist metal into jewelry, serving spoons, andirons, door latches, scissors, combs, toys, and a host of other useful or ornamental objects.

Calder's penchant for tinkering was joined to a solid under-

20

The Red Devil still guards the grounds of Calder's studio at Saché, France

Calder roars along with his circus lion.

Constellation (opposite), a surprisingly intimate wood sculpture, fits in perfectly with the traditional décor of a private home in New York City. As this piece demonstrates, Calder was not only a maker of public monuments and amusing diversions but also a creator of subtle and timeless small sculptures.

Calder's circus delights crowds; a film of the artist running the circus is part of the exhibition.

standing of how things work. In 1919 he was graduated from the Stevens Institute of Technology in Hoboken, New Jersey, with a degree in mechanical engineering. This training helped him achieve the delicate balances and subtle patterns of activity in his motorized and air-powered mobiles. As an engineer he also knew how to make massive metal constructions that would withstand the rigors of time and the elements.

Heroic sculptor, tinkerer, engineer—all of these descriptions fit Calder but none suggests how playful he could be. A few years after college Calder had a job in New York as a newspaper illustrator. With his press pass he gained free admission for two weeks to the Ringling Brothers and Barnum and Bailey Circus—and this experience shaped the rest of his career. In the mid-1920's he created his own circus and entertained the elite of the Paris and New York art world with performances of his miniature animals, clowns, and stuntsmen. Until 1931 he continued to add figures to the circus and it always remained for him a fount of inspiration; as late as 1975 he was turning out new gouaches on circus themes.

His best-known works, of course, are the abstract sculptures he made after 1930. As Calder remarked, "My entrance into the field of abstract art came about as the result of a visit to the studio of Piet Mondrian in Paris in 1930. I was particularly impressed by some rectangles of color he had tacked on his wall in a pattern after his nature. I told him I would like to make them oscillate—he objected."

Calder, fortunately, ignored the objection and went on to invent a whole new genre of oscillating abstractions—the mobile. Mobiles were remarkable not only because they moved but also because they were made of brightly colored metal; when Calder first began his mobiles, traditional materials such as bronze and marble were the accepted media for sculpture. Despite his status as an innovator, Calder refused to take himself—or his new form of art—too seriously: once, when asked how he could tell a mobile was finished, he replied, "When it's time for dinner."

For half a century he functioned as a versatile master rivaled in productivity only by Picasso. Calder designed fountains, tapestries, stage sets, dinner plates, wallpaper, sidewalks, hammocks—and in 1973 he began to paint jets for Braniff. Year after year new works (including some two thousand mobiles) poured out of Calder's two studios—in Roxbury, Connecticut, and Saché in southern France. Last fall, just before he died, Calder took to Washington the model for a combination mobile-stabile that will be installed in the Senate Office Building; last year he also designed a mobile for a new wing of Washington's National Gallery. In February a model of his *Salute to Mexico* was unveiled by that country's first lady, and this spring a stabile is to be placed on Mount Herzl above Jerusalem—Calder's gift to the people of Israel.

His sources of inspiration were manifold. Some works he patterned on the cosmos ("The underlying sense of form in my work," he said, "has been the system of the Universe, or part thereof"). Others were derived from the shapes of nature and bear such titles as *Performing Seal*, *Rat*, *Whale*, *Spider*, *Snow Flurry*, *Bougainvillea*, and *Cucaracha*. All are magical. As his friend the French writer Jacques Prévert once remarked, "He gives pleasure, that's his secret."

Wyeth's Siri: Order and Emotion

ARNOLD NEWMAN

Andrew Wyeth, now fifty-nine, lives next to this renovated mill in Pennsylvania; he spends each summer in Cushing, Maine, where he met Siri Erickson.

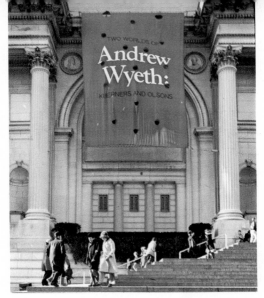

A billowing banner announces the Wyeth show at New York's Metropolitan Museum.

The star of Andrew Wyeth's retrospective at the Metropolitan Museum last winter was *The Virgin*, a vigorous and radiant nude—one of only a few female nudes ever painted by the artist. Virtually ignored by the critics, who always find much to carp about whenever Wyeth's work is shown, *The Virgin* made its appearance in New York and then returned to the quiet of the Brandywine River Museum in Chadds Ford, Pennsylvania. There it hangs in a room with five other Wyeth paintings of Siri Erickson, the daughter of a Finnish neighbor of Wyeth's in Maine.

In the fall of 1967, when Siri was thirteen, Wyeth sketched her standing in a doorway on the Erickson farm. He was fascinated by her towheaded beauty, and later that year he was reminded of her again, when he was in Maine for the funeral of his old friend Christina Olson, the subject of many of his best-known paintings. As he followed the hearse to the funeral, Wyeth remembers passing the Ericksons' house and thinking that Siri was there. Suddenly he realized that Christina Olson's death meant the end of a period in his life and art, and at that moment Siri seemed to symbolize "a rebirth of something fresh out of death." He resolved to paint her when he returned to Maine the following spring.

His six paintings of Siri, here reproduced together for the first time, are particularly precious to Wyeth. On the following pages is Wyeth's account, as told to Thomas Hoving, of how he painted Siri and how the paintings, most especially *The Virgin*, sum up the essentials of his art—emotion tempered by technique.

The paintings of Siri hang in the Brandywine River Museum, near Wyeth's Pennsylvania home.

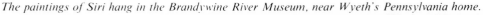

The Brandywine River Museum, above and below, opened almost six years ago in a converted grist mill. The collection includes paintings and drawings by Andrew Wyeth as well as works by his father, N. C. Wyeth; his son, Jamie; his sister and brother-in-law, Henriette and Peter Hurd; and his sister Carolyn. In 1975 a group of patrons gave the paintings of Siri Erickson to the museum, which will soon have available a limited edition of signed color reproductions of the series.

"Not a figure, but a burst of life"
Wyeth's Own Story of Siri

"I went to the Erickson farm and talked to George Erickson and Mrs. Erickson and told them I would love to do a portrait of their daughter. . . . I said I'd like to paint her picture someplace on the farm, perhaps in the barn. I went back the next day. Erickson told me that he thought it would be best to do it in the sauna, since it wasn't used. It was an excellent spot since it was right in front of the house near a clump of beautiful pine trees. I told him that was fine, wonderful. Siri was there looking lovely with her high-colored skin and very long hair. I told her we would go out to the sauna and she cleaned and swept it up the next day.

"I made a drawing of her by the window sitting there with a towel around her. At first I made two drawings of her head, very quickly, and I was thinking about it and the next day I went back, and suddenly I had this brainstorm—well, I thought, here we were in this sauna. I thought with her damp hair, we just might act as if this were a real sauna—a working sauna—with heat. And she told me that she often sat in there anyway and she came out with a towel wrapped around her over her breasts with her shoulders bare. I started a full drawing. I took it home and I was very excited about it. I've never told this story before. I showed [my wife] Betsy the drawing. She thought it was remarkable, terrific; she said, 'You really caught the girl, looking directly at you, no off-looking or looking away.' Here was a young, fourteen-year-old girl, looking you clear in the eye, with blue eyes and damp hair, hands clenched, wonderful strong shoulders, solid knees, and with her feet placed firmly side by side. Betsy said, 'It's a shame you couldn't get her to take off that towel.' I said, 'George Erickson maybe will shoot me, you know she's fourteen years old.'

"But Betsy put the seed in my mind. That's all I needed. So I went back and I started to draw the thing on a panel. Then I asked her, 'Siri, would you pose without the towel around the upper part of your body?' 'Sure,' she said, and she started to take it away and I said, 'Wait a minute, you go and ask your parents, because this can be a rather tricky thing.' She said, 'It's strange you said that, because Daddy said last night, if he's going to do you in a sauna bath, why do you have a towel around you?' Well, that was very encouraging. She came back, she said, 'Fine,' but her father wasn't there at the time and she asked her mother. I thought her father, too, had cleared it. Anyway, I sat there, and she said, 'Close your eyes.' I shut my eyes, and she said, 'Now you can look' and there she was. She was flustered for a few minutes and finally it meant nothing. . . .

"I was already thinking of another painting which I had already entitled *The Virgin*. Later, it turned out to be a shocking picture to people. I think it's because they had built up an image of me at odds with *The Virgin*. That picture shocked the hell out of people. . . . [Siri] was fifteen. That was a remarkable experience because by that time she'd really become a young woman. I did the painting in the Erickson barn and started it on a foggy day. I said to her, 'Come on, Siri, we're going to do this.' She said, 'Well, you stay downstairs.' And she went upstairs in the barn and then came down those steps — a remarkable girl. It was an amazing experience with the quality and the smells of the barn, and this healthy Finnish girl, no affectation, no lipstick, never had had any dates, absolute virgin. It was remarkable, like finding a young doe in the woods. I consider that picture a very precious picture to me because I knew I was looking at something that was untouched, unaffected. Here's a girl who only had outside privies, who had slept all her life in a room on a mattress where the snow could drift in across it. She was healthy, vital, and an intelligent girl, too.

"I worked for about four weeks just on the proportions of her standing figure. You will notice there's no real location again. You're looking down at the feet and up to the head at the same time. You couldn't get that angle with a photograph. She moved in different positions to get the right pose. I wasn't particularly located in any spot. There is a floor there in the painting, but it isn't there, in a sense. I started working on the body and began to paint it in. The sun came out one day, in the morning, and she stepped back, you notice the windows across a barn door. The sun came through them, and her head just hit the sun, which fell against her face and upper body for a short time. I painted like mad. She stepped up the steps a little just to catch that, and it made the picture. It has a marvelous bit of gold with the rest of the room in the shadow. That's what happened, simple as that. . . .

"I really like the painting because it has a kind of mythical quality. Do you know *Pohjola's Daughter* by Sibelius, which to me is an amazing composition? It all goes with that. She once told me she liked to ride bareback in the summer at nighttime

THE SAUNA

BLACK WATER

SEABED

Wyeth first painted Siri Erickson, top, in the sauna on her family's farm in Maine. The last of the series, bottom, was done in 1972, when she was eighteen. That year Wyeth also painted the only water color of the group, center; the other five are tempera.

SIRI

INDIAN SUMMER

Wyeth's one painting of Siri clothed, top, has her in a blouse that picks up the colors of her blond hair, rosy cheeks, and blue eyes. Painting Siri in the nude, first in a barn, opposite, later against a background of trees, above, was "a virginal idea for me, fresh, untouched, with this golden glow about it," Wyeth recalls. "She was powerful. I was in the right spot. It was a bit of luck."

completely nude with her blond hair streaming behind her. It's wild country back there. I used to think about that story and about that amazing figure. This healthy, young Finnish girl on the horse. I even thought of her connection with moose, in terms of the early Finnish legend about an elk and a beautiful girl and the combination of the two. You see all of this came into it. It's a world all of its own. I never consider it a nude painting. I consider it more than that. . . .

"One thing happened during it that came as a great shock to me. I was painting one day and suddenly I could see her staring intently out of the crack of this door. All of a sudden, she rushed out, grabbed a club, and killed a groundhog that had gotten into her father's garden and was eating the vegetables. She just clubbed it to death. Terrific. Blood spattered a little on her legs. Now this is really true, it is her background. She's an earthy girl, God. . . .

"*The Virgin* started off as a much bigger panel. For a while there were baskets of corn hanging above which you use for seed corn in the spring and some stalls with hay. All that was in it for a time, but in the end I cut the panel way down to make it a much better composition. I realized that the emphasis was just right at that cut-down size. I had to go through the other things that were familiar to me before finally I had the guts to put down something fresh. I was relying on the strict disciplinarian side of my nature and then I broke out of that into the freer side by focusing in. Artistically, I went from complexity to simplicity. Within myself I went from the disciplinarian side to the free side.

"Somehow I can't imagine that picture being dated. Maybe the slight mark of the bikini might, but I doubt it, it's so subtle. You wouldn't notice it unless you looked close. And I love that strange line around her that outlines the body. I think it's some of the purest tempera painting I ever did in that torso, because it almost becomes an abstraction of the truth. There are parts of the picture that are almost water color. But I thought this is the flash in the picture. This is the sparkle. . . .

"To me, these pictures of the young Siri are continuations of Olsons, and at the same time they are sharp counteractions to the portraits of Christina, which symbolize the deterioration and the dwindling of something. Then you get suddenly this change of such an invigorating, zestful, powerful phenomenon. Here was something bursting forth, like spring coming through the ground. In a way this was not a figure, but more a burst of life. I don't think it lives just because it's a nude girl. That wasn't the reason at all for painting it. . . . Here, as always, I try to go beyond the subject. That's the summation of my art. Emotion is my bulwark. I think that's the only thing that endures, finally. If you are emotionally involved, you're not going to be easily changed. But if it's purely a technical experience, that's going to be very short-lived. Both technical and emotional have got to be on even terms to be good. . . .

"Art, to me, is seeing. I think you have got to use your eyes as well as your emotion, and one without the other just doesn't work. That's my art." ☐

Dancing in the Seventies

Discos have revived what rock music killed.
The beat is loud, the movements
frenzied, but the scene is very laid back

By JAMAKE HIGHWATER

Saint Vitus has appeared and disappeared in history with mysterious regularity, but no one has successfully explained either his dominion in some ages or his absence from others. The dancing epidemics of Germany and Italy in the Middle Ages have been blamed on everything from mildew in the rye meal to religious fanaticism. But one thing is certain: in every age dance madness has swept whole cultures, even those that are usually sedate.

Saint Vitus was a central force in the ancient Roman Bacchanalia, in the infectious waltzes that swept Europe in the nineteenth century; he was the hypnotic pulse behind the Charleston in the twenties, the lindy in the thirties, the jitterbug in the forties and fifties. And he set the style for the dance eccentricity that became the hallmark of the frenetic 1960's: the Twist, Hully-Gully, Boogaloo, Fish, Monkey, Bug, Frug, Pony, Mashed Potatoes, Fly, Funky Chicken, Jerk, Watusi, Hitchhike, Freeze, Wobble, Locomotion, and dozens of other overnight sensations. Then at the end of the sixties, the rock concert hall or stadium took the place of the ballroom and the dancing stopped.

But not for long. Saint Vitus is back.

Radical then: Snake Hips Tucker's slither and Presley's pelvic thrust

He has toppled the jazz, rock, and folk superstars whose fans didn't like to dance and has become king of thousands of discos, which today seem to be more numerous across America than hamburger joints.

The discotheque was a French invention that came to America in the early sixties. After a brief flurry of success, discotheques went out of fashion. By the late sixties the few discos in America were scorned as relics of a former flashy lifestyle. If nothing else was certain in those rebellious years, it was clear that the world was divided into "us" and "them." What really mattered was not the dance steps but the lyrics, which only the young understood:

Semolina pilchard climbing up
   the Eiffel Tower.
Element'ry penguin singing
   Hare Krishna man you should
   have seen them kicking Edgar
   Allan Poe.
I am the eggman, they are the
   eggmen—I am the walrus
   Goo Goo Goo Joob Goo
   Goo Goo Joob Goo Goo
   GooooooooooooJooooob.*

Originally rock had been a robust and admittedly primitive music played by near amateurs. At their first concert the Jefferson Airplane had only four tunes, which they played over and over again. Then groups such as Cream introduced jazzlike improvisation to the music. Gradually the era of rock critics and serious fans began, and people sat down on the huge dance floors (or in auditoriums) and listened to the pyrotechnical displays of professional musicians. At first it was all right if a few people continued to get up and boogie, but eventually such dancing was frowned upon as the antics of exhibitionist clowns and clods.

Meanwhile in Europe the discotheques thrived. In Amsterdam, in Rome, and especially in Paris fashionably dressed couples—who wouldn't be

*"I Am the Walrus" by John Lennon and Paul McCartney. © 1967, Northern Songs, Ltd.

Chic now: gyrations of Princess Yasmin, Ali Khan's daughter, at Regine's in New York

seen dead in denim and boots—trotted elegantly if rather woodenly across dance floors in steps that looked like a cross between the polka and the lindy. The sixties had no influence on these Europeans; they never really learned to use their bodies when they danced.

When the rock era ended in the early seventies, it was a fortunate return to normalcy for some. For others it was the triumph of mediocrity. Critics saw the rise of the discos as the decline of political involvement and alternative lifestyles. And the new music—the music of the discos—records played loudly by jockeys with a mania for manipulating their audience—satisfied nothing but the feet. The beat is a straight, soulless 4/4 without any of the subtle inner rhythms that made rock so sensual and complex. The lyrics are pointless at best, tasteless at worst. In "Disco Duck" by Rick Dees and His Cast of Idiots, the words *disco duck* are repeated endlessly by Donald Duck voices. Dancers cavort to such songs with blank faces, untouched by the mindless lyrics.

Disco sound has not always been like that. Labelle, a three-woman group, now defunct, graced the early dance era with "Lady Marmalade," and singer Gloria Gaynor has had a few appealing tunes. But on the whole the highly overproduced disco sound has lost all energy as well as every trace of freshness and invention. Rock was

noted for its directness and uncluttered instrumentation. When the Beatles used a classical string quartet in "Yesterday," strings were unheard of in rock. Now waves of lush string accompaniment pour over the meager melodies and attempt to elevate unimaginative twelve-bar songs. This emphasis upon arrangement has caused a recycling of old standards from previous eras, souped up and churned through a rhythm machine. The bands serve up a Hustle-beat version of "I've Got You under My Skin," an outrage to anybody who ever liked swing. The trend of giving oldies a face-lift has continued unabated: one of the biggest disco hits of 1976 was a number called "A Fifth of Beethoven" by Walter Murphy's Big Apple Band. You can never tell where the next sensation will come from. One current success is the music of an ex-porn queen's group called Andrea True Connection.

Whereas rock came essentially from England and California, the disco sound was born in New York out of a combination of black and Latin music. Like rock, it has its admirers and critics. David Todd, the baron disc jockey who reigns at Manhattan's Jouissance Disco, likes it because "it really makes you want to dance." Pop critic Peter Occhiogrosso disagrees: "The disco sound reduces music to an automated beat, packaged string arrangements,

cooing girl-choruses, and everything else that the classic FM-radio format of the sixties most loathed about AM-radio music. It's the pits! It's the triumph of plastic!"

Whatever the merits of the music, the discos themselves have their own ambiance. Their atmosphere and architecture range from rich to raunchy. Perhaps one of the most magical discos is on the island of Sardinia, where the Aga Khan turned a primitive string of beaches into the magnificent Costa Smeralda. Tucked amid all this wealth and splendor is a disco called Rituel, a glistening white cave shaped like an amphitheatre, with successive tiers etched into the rock walls and strewn with hundreds of white pillows, upon which the rich recline in splendiferous near nudity. A slowly turning light machine fills the cave with vivid colored images, and at the lowest level of the cavern, on a tiny dance floor of ebony marble, gorgeous people move ever so slightly, with their eyes closed, to a hurricane of rhythmic music. If, God forbid, they should perspire, there is a rustic terrace reached through a hole in the cave's ceiling. From that lofty perch they can turn their brows toward sea breezes while they watch the moon over the calm Mediterranean.

Not so choice are discos where flashing lights and thumping music create an atmosphere that is as drab as a roadhouse, where, in the rest rooms, guys labor over their locks and play John Garfield to the mirror while their dates primp in the powder room.

But whatever their tone and style, however reactionary or mindless in the view of critics, discos have achieved a certain sociological importance. They are possibly the only public places where the major forces of the sixties' rebellion have had a lasting impact.

Social historians frequently point out that only two characteristics of the last decade—the new sensibilities regarding sex and race—have retained their influence. In the dance palaces of the seventies the complicated social scheme epitomizes avant-garde sexual and racial ideas. The young dance maniacs have so assimilated novel forms of behavior that they are scarcely aware of them.

The dance hall has always been the most conspicuous testing ground for sexual manners—and following tradition, discos provide a place where new attitudes about sex roles can be freely played out. In the seventies the idea of couples is so casually treated that single women can enjoy themselves in discos without the slightest stigma. Slow dancing to romantic numbers is regaining popularity, and the renewed interest in contact dancing has brought about a renovation of the lindy and the jitterbug called the Hustle—a rather tame little dance in which the partners hold hands and pace stridently (with almost no torsal movement) through a succession of solo and duetted turns.

But none of the contact dancing has put an end to the typical improvisations of the sixties: people get up and dance alone or in groups, and members of the same sex also dance together. Here, in the dancing of men with each other and of women with each other, the disco represents a really drastic change in social convention and sexual attitudes.

It is neither a secret nor an excuse for gossip that some of the best discos in America and Europe were started as gay establishments that began to open their doors to anyone who wanted to dance. Five years ago Le Sept, an elegant gay disco in Paris, was considered among the ten best nightspots of Europe. The fact that some discos are gay or "mixed" is casually noted in night-life features of the major newspapers, which take for granted freedoms that until very recently were the basis of scandal.

Although sex has often been perceived as a reality behind the ballroom, race has not. But there is no question that during the last decade black people's attitudes about dancing suddenly and completely changed the way that white people danced. The new sensualization of body movement was absolutely revolutionary, making a significant connection between dance, race, and sexuality. Nothing can ever be quite the same again.

To find someone who personifies all of these dramatic changes in American society we must go back to a white man from Mississippi named Elvis Presley. There was a rich black heritage behind everyone who grew up in Mississippi—whether he liked it or not. So Elvis knew about a dancer named Earl "Snake Hips" Tucker even though he had probably never heard his name. It was all part of "jukin'," putting a nickel in the juke box and letting your body go.

And Elvis knew about Perry Bradford, an old black man born in 1890 in Atlanta. He was part of jukin' too. "Touring the south in them early days," Bradford once said, "I saw a million steps in a million tonks. The dancers had all kinds of names and no names for them, and I just took over the steps I liked and put them in my act. Once in a while, if the step went over big, I'd work up a tune and lyrics that explained how to do it, have it printed, and sell it to the audience after my act."

That was probably the beginning of the whole dance craze that later swept America, and that is how elements of vernacular dance surfaced as sheet music. "The publishers wouldn't take no songs from colored people then," Bradford explained, "so I had them printed privately and sold them for a nickel apiece in theatres."

When Elvis emerged from all that unconscious, rich tradition, he was strutting in the shadow of dancers like King Rastus Brown and Bill Robinson, Frank Condos and James Barton, Harland Dixon and John W. Bubbles. If Presley's musical success was beholden to blues singer Arthur "Big Boy" Crudup and to songwriter Otis Blackwell, he owed most of his initial fame as a performer to his dancemasters: a whole tribe of black men from minstrel shows and carnivals, circuses and key clubs, tonks and Apollo shows.

Rock and television grew up together, and Elvis caused the crisis on the tube that finally broke the boycott of race music—as the music of blacks was known in those days. Producers had previously sold a certain amount of black music and dance in films and on television by "whitewashing" the performers or reducing their acts to Amos and Andy buffoonery. But Elvis, although he sometimes behaved like a

Labelle: glitter, gospel, and soul

black man, was a white man, and he was a sufficient hit in the south to gain an appearance on national television. With Elvis's success on the Ed Sullivan show, the commercial union of television and rock was born.

It was never the rockabilly music that Presley sang that bothered people; it was his dancing. "I gotta move," he said. "When I sing I gotta move." Elvis was genuinely hurt by the criticism of his performances, and he once asked his mother if she thought his movements were really obscene. She replied, "Course not, sonny . . . trouble with you is that you jest work too hard when you're singin'."

Actually Presley's motions were a relatively tame version of the dance popularized in Harlem nightclubs during the twenties by performers like Snake Hips Tucker. Tucker was known in the hard-boiled language of show business as a freak dancer. He came into the New York music world of Connie's Inn and the Cotton Club by way of the tidewaters of Maryland, and he worked for a short time with Duke Ellington, who described his famous performance: Tucker wore a loose white silk blouse with large puffed sleeves, tight black pants with bell bottoms, and a sequined girdle with a sparkling buckle, from which hung a large glittery tassel. His menacing look gave his audience the feeling that he was a cobra and they were mice. He slithered on stage and at once everyone quieted down. He came slipping and sliding forward with just a hint of hip movement, establishing the kinetic theme of his fantastic dance. Gradually as the shining buckle threw out reflections of light in large circles and the tassel swung into action, the embarrassed audience realized that the dancer's whole torso was becoming increasingly involved in his movements.

The audience, especially the women, were always impressed by the act, and when Tucker briefly appeared on Broadway in *Blackbirds of 1928*, the press expressed shock: "such coarse suggestiveness should be eliminated!"

The hassle was with the tassel. It was

Dr. Buzzard's Original Savannah Band: upbeat forties' "dua, dua"

that way in the twenties for Earl Tucker and it was that way in the fifties for Elvis Presley. By the sixties, however, pelvic dancing caused no outrage and superstars who specialized in it became millionaires.

The sixties was not the first time that white kids had tried to dance like blacks. In the forties they had painstakingly learned the most acrobatic jitterbug, but their performances were always dull in comparison to those of the expressive black dancers. Behind the white man's inarticulate body was a puritanical condemnation of dancing, and it was not easy to reverse the repression of centuries. When Elvis and other performers made the cavorting of people like Snake Hips Tucker attractive rather than offensive to thousands upon thousands of young white Americans, they accomplished a definitive cultural and racial change. And the fundamental alteration in the American way of thinking about the body—and about the kind of gestures appropriate to males and females, blacks or whites—has culminated in the discos of the seventies.

It is possible that the disco world is as representative of the seventies as Woodstock was of its era. And the disco sound is becoming more sophisticated and is winning new converts. One group from Manhattan, Dr. Buzzard's Original Savannah Band, is popular now on both the East and West coasts. In New York people are dancing to the Savannah Band's witty songs at discos like Jouissance, Infinity, and 12 West, in super-priced Regine's on Park Avenue, and in the pimp-and-player bars off Forty-

second Street. In Los Angeles the Savannah Band's hit "Cherchez la Femme" booms at the Bullshot and Studio I. Disco dancers are a very mixed crowd—gay and straight, young and middle-aged, black and white—and the music, too, is an amalgam of twenties' and thirties' dance-band mannerisms, pop countermelodies, and occasional dissonances, all moving to a Hustle beat through a beautiful sound system. There is something in disco—its combination of musical styles from several eras, its nostalgic forties' drag and camp hair styles, and even its mindlessness—that appeals to many people of different kinds and different ages.

Disco is a kind of mentality—for better or for worse. It is what pumps life and success into the performances of the sassy avant-garde dance group led by Twyla Tharp, who makes an entrance doing a slow drag. Disco fabricates a new cool lifestyle and gives it a place to live. This new cool is made up of equal parts frenzy, apathy, and fatalism—a bit like the last tango on the good ship *Titanic*. When August Darnell, the songwriter for the Savannah Band, was asked in the midst of the utter bedlam of a disco to define the new style, he glanced slowly among the bobbing bodies, the expressionless faces, and the feathered-and-denimed fashion show, and answered: "Wellllll, it's a matter of how laid back you can be without falling asleep." □

Jamake Highwater is a contributing editor of Stereo Review *and the author of* Rock and Other Four-Letter Words.

The Disco Beat

It is one A.M., and the disco is just filling up. Recent arrivals —a solitary woman in a metallic tube top, a twosome in tennis shorts and orange caps, a male pair in satin jump suits—drift toward the dance floor, a cavernous space drenched by sound from a dozen overhead speakers and riddled with multicolored strobes. Here for a night anyone can be a star—mouthing lyrics, glistening under spotlights, showing off bralessness or biceps. Discos are a place for letting go—and exhibitionism.

In an elevated enclosure a DJ wearing earphones times the smooth transitions from one turntable to another and orchestrates the lights. The disc he spins is hot; the spots flash crimson and purple; the floor pulsates as hordes of dancers—maybe four or five hundred on a Saturday— bounce, sway, shimmy, and rock through steps with no names or some version of the Hustle.

A mustachioed man in a white "Clyde" suit shoulders a Lolita in black lace, flails his arms, and whoops out lyrics: "Dazz, dazz, disco dazz/ Dazz, dazz, disco . . ."* A large bedenimed girl swirls with a middle-aged woman dressed in an argyle sweater and cashmere skirt, blue-gray to match her tinted hair. An Edwardian pair—he in a pale yellow collarless shirt and vest, she in ivory eyelet and pink ribbons —throbs in a close embrace. Stragglers float through the pungent air—tobacco tinged with perfume and pot— toward seats near the mirrored walls. A microskirted mannequin glimpses the reflection of a rangy black man. His shirt draped over his outstretched arms, he has been soaring around the room in ever-smaller concentric circles. Now he orbits around her.

Fourteen (or is it forty?) songs later it's five A.M., and clutches of sated revelers glide outside to the empty street. No one sees those who spent the night being seen.

*"Dazz" by R. Ransom, R. Hargis, and E. Iroas. ©1975 and 1976, Silver Cloud Music and Trolley Music.

From his cubicle a DJ programs revels and promotes discs—a smash may have 200,000 copies sold before it is even heard on radio. Here and on the following pages are disco patrons in New York and Los Angeles.

PAST PERFECT

Man and Friend at Yale

Paul Mellon is not only a great collector of art but also an avid horse breeder (he has a large horse farm in Upperville, Virginia). Small wonder, then, that the Mellon collection of British paintings includes an unrivaled group of animal and sporting pictures. The full extent of the collection was announced at the opening last month of the Yale Center for British Art. The center, which Mellon gave to his alma mater, houses some eighteen hundred paintings (including major works by Constable, Turner, and Hogarth), about five thousand prints, seven thousand drawings, and sixteen thousand rare books—a comprehensive survey of British culture from the sixteenth to the nineteenth century. The four-story building with a façade of glass and stainless steel is itself a work of art; it was Louis Kahn's last design before his death in 1974.

Standouts even in this stellar crowd are the animal pictures. No subject for a painting was dearer to the heart of an eighteenth-century English aristocrat than his horses or his hunting dogs (typically, the ninth earl of Pembroke left elaborate instructions in his will for the care of his horses, and when he was still alive, his correspondents always begged to be remembered to Fop and Chuff—the earl's dogs). In the Mellon collection are many eighteenth-century paintings of mounted sportsmen with titles such as *Thomas Mellish on Saucebox* and *John Corbet, Sir Robert Leighton and Sir J. Kynaston with Their Horses and Hounds.*

The supreme animal artist of the period was George Stubbs (1724–1806), a self-taught painter who could capture the elegant anxiety of a *White Poodle in a Boat* or the touching dignity of a *Zebra* (an African rarity that apparently belonged to the young George III). Stubbs, represented at the center by thirty-five works, became so obsessed with animals that for him they were the measure rather than the mere possessions of human beings—as is evident from the title of his last book, *Comparative Anatomical Exposition of the Human Body with That of a Tiger and a Common Fowl.*

See It Now

A new museum has opened in the middle of Manhattan where visitors can view and study thousands of artifacts once displayed in their own homes. This is the Museum of Broadcasting, endowed by CBS chairman William

Sitting at a console, a visitor to the Museum of Broadcasting in Manhattan reruns a historic interview of Carl Sandburg.

Paley to preserve the gems and ordinary milestones of the two talking media.

The "artifacts" are cassettes of radio and television programs from all the networks, taken from the first fifty years of American broadcasting. Stored on an unseen floor, the tapes are catalogued in a card library and can be played back on any of eight Sony color video machines in a thickly carpeted room called the Broadcast Service Center. There, seated at an enclosed console and wearing headphones, visitors can listen to Amos and Andy rant about Sapphire, visit Carl Sandburg as Edward R. Murrow did in 1954, pass through the White House with Jackie Kennedy or Harry Truman, watch the Watergate hearings all over again, or scrutinize the various apologies and denials of Richard Nixon.

Mostly the museum recalls great events, such as the John F. Kennedy funeral, the first moon walk, and Jimmy Carter's inau-

guration. But for sheer interest or entertainment, a 1964 trip to the Louvre with Charles Boyer is available, as is the Rod Serling play *Requiem for a Heavyweight*, aired in 1956. Students of politics would want to hear the crackling voice of Herbert Hoover as he delivered a campaign speech in Cleveland on October 15, 1932. Or they could re-view CBS's controversial documentary "The Selling of the Pentagon," shown in 1971. And what would a broadcasting archives be without Orson Welles's "War of the Worlds" radio hoax on Halloween eve, 1938? Overall, some two thousand programs—including commercials—are just waiting to be put back on the air, with another two thousand to be added by the end of the year.

Heritage on Stage

Roots, Alex Haley's re-creation of black history, has a powerful counterpart in the world of dance. *Blood Memories*, a new

George Stubbs's Zebra *is a prize pet in the new Mellon collection at Yale.*

fifty-minute ballet choreographed by Donald McKayle and performed by Alvin Ailey's American Dance Theater, takes its inspiration from these lines by Langston Hughes: "I've known rivers:/ I've known rivers ancient as the world and older than the flow of human blood in human veins./ My soul has grown deep like the rivers."

The rivers that flow through *Blood Memories* are the Nile, the Mississippi, and the Harlem. In each sequence the tall and magnificently sinuous Judith Jamison moves as the soul of the rivers. The Nile sequence celebrates the prowess of black warriors as well as the peaceful, nurturing rhythms of the life of a farmer and his young bride. The Mississippi scenes, by contrast, express the more destructive forces of nature. A delta flood wipes out whole families, and the survivors migrate north. But Harlem is no refuge. Ghetto blacks are driven to anger and despair, and one derelict drowns, symbolically, in the polluted waters. The ballet ends as a young man in Harlem assimilates the pastoral experience of Africa and the terror of the Mississippi flood, and he discovers a new strength in his heritage.

One critic hailed *Blood Memories*, Alvin Ailey's biggest production ever, as "a monumental endeavor," though others criticized its complex scenario. No matter. It is one of the most popular works performed by the Ailey troupe in its tour of fourteen cities this winter and spring. Evoking the past in vivid and poetic fashion, it represents, as does *Roots*, part of a new awareness of and feeling for the African experience of black Americans.

Up

While the stock market has been backing and filling, everything's coming up dollars in the auction market. Some record prices set in 1976 at Sotheby Parke Bernet in New York:

• Paul Gauguin's oil painting *Still Life with Japanese Print* brought $1.4 million, an increase of $450,000 over the previous top for a Gauguin.

• Four lithographs by Francisco Goya, *The Bulls of Bordeaux*, sold for $160,000, a record for such works by the Spanish artist.

• A ruby ring, mounted in platinum and diamonds, fetched a stunning $31,700 for each of its seven and a quarter carats—a total of $230,000, the highest per-ruby-carat price ever.

• Ming jars are not exactly rarities at art auctions, but a splendid one broke all records for Chinese art sold in this country, going for $260,000.

• A 1931 canvas by Edward Hopper, *Hotel Room*, brought $200,000. It was the first major

Hopper oil sold at auction and thus established a norm for his works.

So far, 1977 continues to be a record-breaking year. A 292-year-old Stradivarius violin

A chair goes from rags to riches.

brought $80,000, while a 125-year-old Heriz silk carpet from Iran went for $200,000, five times its presale estimate.

But the real highs of 1977 have been racked up by early American furniture. Two Queen Anne chairs from pre-Revolutionary Philadelphia brought $140,000—$50,000 more than any previously auctioned pair. And a carved Chippendale wing chair, also from Philadelphia, set a record $85,000. It has flawless carving, but when the auctioneer said, "Going, going, gone," the bidders thought he meant the upholstery.

Italian Pessimism

Last year American moviegoers got a chilling view of survival during World War II: Lina Wertmuller's *Seven Beauties*, a film about a Neapolitan petty criminal who makes it through the war and concentration camp by relinquishing all moral principles. Now another account of World War II, also by an Italian woman, has just been published here. It is *History*, a novel by Elsa Morante that caused a sensation in Italy when it was first published in 1974. Like Wertmuller, Morante portrays her characters as victims of history, but unlike Wertmuller's anti-hero, Morante's poor family struggling for survival in Rome is finally ground down by the forces set against it. At the book's conclusion, in the year 1947, all the major characters have died in misery.

Morante's novel is also a work of history, reflecting the double meaning of *la storia* in Italian: "story" and "history." Interspersed among the fictional episodes are passages about world events, starting in 1901. At the beginning of the book, describing the years 1906–13, she sets the tone for her "factual" narrative: "Nothing very new in the great world. Like all the centuries and the millennia that have preceded it on earth, the new century also observes the well-known, immobile principle of historical dynamics: power to some, servitude to the others."

Morante, who is a self-proclaimed anarchist, once wrote her personal manifesto: "Since her birth the author has been an anarchist; in other words she considers the domination of some people over others—be it financial, ideological, military, familial or any other, of whatever origin, form or pretext—the most gloomy, hideous and shameful thing on earth."

History, as fiction and fact, emphasizes the gloom and shame of human events to an extraordinary degree; yet Morante's view struck a responsive chord among Italians, who have bought more copies (some 600,000) of her book than of any other recent work by an Italian.

Lovers dance a tender pas de deux beside the Nile (symbolized by Judith Jamison in the background) in Blood Memories.

Why Men and Women Think Differently

It's not only social conditioning, after all.
New research shows that the brains of males and females are not alike
and are intended to perform in different ways

The protein deficiency disorder called kwashiorkor is found among people whose daily diet is restricted to such starchy foods as corn, cassava, and sweet potatoes. In the course of the disease, which is often fatal, the victim's liver malfunctions. Among male sufferers, the liver no longer inactivates the estrogen—the female sex hormone—normally produced by the male sex glands, and as a result, afflicted boys and men soon find that their breasts swell like a pubescent girl's. Males feminized by kwashiorkor not only begin to resemble women biologically but, as a psychologist discovered in the late 1960's, they also begin to think like women—which is to say, when tested they showed lower spatial ability, lower numerical ability, and greater verbal ability.

These observations are in conflict with our way of thinking about these matters, for it is currently fashionable to suggest that the commonly observed differences in the intellectual capabilities of men and women are determined by social conditioning rather than by biology. Our up-to-date conventional wisdom tells us that intellectual ability is distributed by nature without regard to sex. The comparatively low numbers of, say, female engineers and mathematicians are taken as evidence of the lack of encouragement and opportunity given to women rather than any lack of particular abilities among them. Yet

within the past five years or so, a sizable body of biological evidence has revived the ancient idea that the brains of men and women are not identical but are specialized and intended to perform in somewhat different ways.

The message that there are distinct differences of brain organization between the sexes—biologically this is an example of dimorphism—is likely to be seized upon by the fiercer feminists as one more attempt to deny woman her rightful place in the world. But, as Corinne Hutt, a psychologist at the Human Development Research Unit at Park Children's Hospital, Oxford, England, has remarked: "The fact that such functional dimorphism exists may be unacceptable to many human females, but denial of it does not prove its absence."

The work currently under way tends to fall into three fields of investigation: (1) the genetic transmission of certain abilities; (2) male/female differences in the development and functioning of the right and left hemispheres of the brain; and (3) the influence of sex hormones on intellectual ability.

Quite apart from their sex organs, infant boys and girls do not arrive in the world with identical physical equipment. To begin with, their experiences in the womb have been different. The male fetus develops more rapidly at first, manifesting its sex four weeks earlier

than the female; after that, the male slows down. By the time they arrive in the world, boy babies are larger but girl babies are more mature. The boy's brain is larger, too, and will continue to be larger as he grows; an average adult male's brain weighs 1,400 grams, an adult woman's weighs 1,260 grams. The newborn girl's nervous system, however, is physically more highly developed.

Infant boys and infant girls also behave differently, in ways that reflect differences in the anatomies of the central nervous systems. According to Hutt, the attention of male infants tends to be caught by visual patterns, while female infants are more attracted by sounds. The boy's physical activity consists largely of startles, while the girl has a repertoire of rhythmic mouthing, smiling, and sucking. On the whole, girls learn to speak earlier and soon move on to relatively sophisticated sentences. As the psychologist Jerome Kagan of Harvard has reported, infant girls also show a livelier anxiety in unfamiliar surroundings.

These differences are necessarily determined by biology, not by the environment, but as each child develops and is shaped not only by his/her genetic heritage but also by his/her experience of the world, the innate differences become obscured. However, we continue to recognize differences in the psychology of men and women regardless of whether

COLLAGES BY JOAN HALL

they have been shaped by biology or social conditioning.

In recent years a prodigious amount of scientific work has been done in identifying psychological differences between men and women—in temperament, social behavior, and power relationships, as well as in general intelligence and capacity for achievement. Eleanor Emmons Maccoby, who heads the department of psychology at Stanford, and her colleague Carol Nagy Jacklin, have undertaken to render this corpus of experimental work intelligible. They read and annotated more than seventeen hundred papers— mainly studies in the psychology of behavior—summarized the results, and then looked through the summaries to see what conclusions they could draw.

They found that many cherished items of folk wisdom were unsupported by the scientific reports, particularly the beliefs that girls, as compared to boys, are more sociable and more suggestible, have lower self-esteem, are better at rote learning, are more affected by heredity, lack achievement motivation, and are less analytical.

But there were some "fairly well established" differences, chiefly that girls

excel in verbal ability while boys excel in visual/spatial and mathematical ability. Boys were also found to be more aggressive. Left as open questions were how the sexes differ in tactile sensitivity, activity levels, competitiveness, dominance, compliance, and nurturance, and also in regard to fear, timidity, and anxiety.

In the end Maccoby and Jacklin concluded that although there are some measurable differences in certain intellectual qualities of men and women, the differences are not at all large, and there is much overlap between the sexes.

Differences in intellectual quality do not necessarily imply differences in intelligence, of course, The argument as to whether men or women are on the whole more intelligent is doomed to remain unsettled for the good reason that nobody has managed to devise a generally acceptable definition of intelligence. According to the *Encyclopaedia Britannica*, "Intelligence is a hypothetical construct used to describe individual differences in an assumed latent variable that is, by any direct means, unobservable and unmeasurable." We continue to test people for their intelligence quotients even as we hear passionate arguments that (1)

whatever the IQ measures is not intelligence at all, and (2) the tests of IQ are culturally biased in favor of middle-class whites. The IQ cannot, however, be thrown out on grounds of being sexually biased; questions that reflected sex differences were removed while the tests were being developed.

Even though we can't usefully compare the differences in overall IQ between men and women, we can learn a good deal from the differences between them in particular abilities. Using a test called the Wechsler Adult Intelligence Scale, Hutt reports that, on the whole, males performed better in the categories labeled (somewhat obscurely) information, comprehension, digit span, arithmetic, block design, picture completion, and object assembly. Females did better on vocabulary, similarities, digit symbol, and picture arrangements. Hutt goes on to challenge the commonly accepted view that women score higher on verbal tests because they are superior in the use of language. Instead, she argues that females are merely more fluent verbally and that this is an entirely different matter from being superior in verbal reasoning. "It is clear," she writes, "that where reasoning or the logical manipulation of concepts or relationships are concerned, males are superior, irrespective of the content of the problem, i.e., numbers, words, patterns."

This opinion receives some support from Maccoby, who suggests that whether the reasons are biological or social, girls' thinking, as compared to that of boys, is "less analytic, more global, and more persevering." She goes on to say that no matter how useful this sort of thinking may be, it is not the kind that leads to high-level intellectual productivity, particularly in science.

Two substantial questions therefore must be tackled without flinching. First, are the differences that have been identified due entirely to social conditioning or are they dictated by differences in biology? Second, if these differences are indeed small, why is it that men have achieved so much more in doing the intellectual work of the world?

Biologically speaking, the essential difference between a man and a woman is that *she* started out with two X-chromosomes and *he* started out with an X-chromosome and a Y-chromosome. Everything else follows from this. The great question is whether differences in the quality of intelligence and in the ability to achieve intellectual work are transmitted with the chromosomes or are developed at home and at school. So far as the male's superior ability to solve spatial problems is concerned, there is good reason to believe that the answer lies in the chromosomes.

A recent study carried out by two American investigators, R. Darrell Bock of the University of Chicago and Donald Kolakowski of the University of Connecticut, analyzed the high scores in tests for spatial ability among 167 suburban families. The results showed clearly that spatial ability had been transmitted in a crisscross fashion— fathers to daughters and mothers to sons—a pattern geneticists recognize as indicating that the trait is being carried by a recessive, sex-linked gene. The researchers argue that "there exists no theory of child development and nurturance which predicts the cross-correlation pattern exhibited. . . . Nor does it appear possible to explain this phenomenon by a genetic mechanism other than sex linkage."

This does not mean that all women are denied the ability to solve spatial problems. It does mean that men and women receive this trait in different proportions—about 50 per cent of men are actually so endowed but only about 25 per cent of women. Maccoby and Jacklin comment on this finding: "To say that there is a genetic component in spatial ability does *not* imply that this ability is something, like male genitals, that men have and women do not."

The fact that women have not made large inroads into fields such as engineering, in which a high degree of spatial ability is needed, is clearly due to something more fundamental than the hostility of male engineers. It is due, in part at least, to biology. We must quickly remind ourselves that the difference is not of kind but of numbers. The women who are spatially gifted are fewer by half than the men, but the quality of their performance is just as high. So far as these individuals are concerned, the averages mean nothing at all.

Our understanding of the average male superiority in spatial thinking and the average female superiority in verbal fluency is strengthened by our growing knowledge about the development of the human brain.

One of the most distinctive features of the brain is that it is divided into two large hemispheres. Curiously, each hemisphere serves the opposite side of the body—the right ear, for example, reporting to the left hemisphere. In recent years, through the study of both normal people and the victims of brain damage, we have learned that the two hemispheres do not perform exactly the same functions. In right-handed people the left hemisphere is dominant for speech and the processing of information that is easily put into words, and the right hemisphere is dominant in the processing of spatial information and other material that is hard to put into words. In left-handed people the functions are reversed.

The specialization of hemispheres appears to develop differently in boys and girls. The lateralization of functions in one hemisphere or the other has been studied with regard to sex differences in both verbal and spatial performance. Doreen Kimura, an experimental psychologist at the University of Southern Ontario, suggests that dominance for speech perception advances more rapidly in the young female brain than in the young male brain. As for spatial ability, Sandra Witelson of the department of psychiatry of McMaster University, Ontario, reported in 1976 that her studies showed that the right hemispheres of boys had become specialized as early as age six, while this specialization was not found to occur with girls until age thirteen or later.

Witelson studied two hundred right-handed children, divided into groups of twenty-five within each two-year interval from six to thirteen years. They were all normal in intelligence, academic progress, and physical development. The test they were given was designed to measure the relative participation of the two hemispheres in processing spatial material. Each child was required to feel simultaneously two shapes that were kept out of sight, feeling one shape with the fingers of the right hand and the other with the fingers of the left hand. After ten seconds of exploration by touch, the child would try to choose the correct shapes from a display. Ten test trials were given each child, with scores recorded for the number of left- and right-hand objects correctly identified.

When the scores were in, it turned out that while there was no difference in overall accuracy between the boys and the girls, the left- and right-hand patterns for the sexes were quite different. The left-hand scores of the boys were significantly higher than their right-hand scores, while there was no left-right difference in the scores of the girls. Witelson interprets this lopsidedness in the boys' scores as meaning that for boys of age six or older the right hemisphere has already become more specialized than the left for processing spatial information. For girls this specialization does not appear until adolescence. Witelson suggests that this "neural dimorphism" between the sexes may be caused not only by genetic differences but also by the effects of sex hormones.

The male sex hormone androgen seems to be the key to heightened intellectual functioning among another group of people. As the result of a genetic fault, some fetuses are exposed to an excess of androgen in the womb. In the male fetus affected by this fault the excess androgen does not cause any visible change in its normal development; the female fetus, however, becomes visibly masculinized, with the external sex organs growing to resemble the male's.

At Johns Hopkins Medical School, John Money and Viola Lewis studied seventy such people ranging in age from two and one-half to forty-eight. A remarkably large number of them turned out to have high IQs—12.9 per cent had IQs of 130 or higher, whereas only 2.2 per cent of the general population would be expected to have IQs this high; 31.5 per cent had IQs over 120 as against the expected 8.9 per cent; and 60.1 per cent had IQs over 110, as against an expected 25 per cent. Furthermore, the IQs of these people were high for all types of tasks, both verbal and spatial.

Money and another colleague, Anke A. Ehrhardt, then went on to investigate another hormonal imbalance in the fetus, this time an excess of progestin, the synthetic pregnancy hormone, which used to be given to prevent miscarriage. Like an excess of androgen, the progestin sometimes caused the female fetus to develop partial or complete male sex organs. Money and Ehrhardt persuaded the parents of ten girls afflicted by progestin-induced female hermaphroditism to let them study their daughters. Six of the ten girls were found to have IQs greater than 130. None fell below 100. The sample is too small for these findings to be conclusive, but the work of the Johns Hopkins researchers is buttressed by similar reports from the Soviet Union and England.

As Money concluded in one of his papers, "It is, of course, still too early to make any sweeping generalizations from these findings. But [British researcher] Katharine Dalton's work, taken together with our own, strongly suggests that androgens, synthetic progestenic hormones and progesterone [the natural pregnancy hormone], given prenatally, do produce an increase in intelligence and eventual academic performance. They do so in both males and females, but only when the fetuses are subjected to the hormone in excess at a critical time of their development in the uterus."

More direct evidence that hormones influence the sexual differentiation of the brain has been reported by Bruce S. McEwen of Rockefeller University, who has located hormone-sensitive cells in the brain and has investigated how they fit into the nerve pathways that govern behavior. Working with newborn rats, McEwen found that if he deprived the males of the male sex hormone testosterone by castrating them, they grew up to display female patterns of behavior. Conversely, if testosterone was given to newborn female rats, they grew up acting like males. (Unlike human brains, the brains of rats do not become sexually differentiated until the first week of life outside the womb, a period during which hormones can have permanent effects on the brain.)

McEwen suggests that testosterone (or its derivative, estradiol) reaches target nerve cells at a time that is critical for the sexual differentiation of the brain. Certain genes are activated, others are suppressed. "As a result," he proposes, "the hormone may influence the pattern of the connections the affected nerve cells form with other nerve cells and thereby may determine the nerve circuits in part of the brain." The important thing to note here is that the change in behavior is produced by a change in the structure of the rats' brains and not merely by the presence or absence of the hormone. McEwen believes that the mechanism involved is found in the development of neurons and the formation of synaptic contacts with other neurons. His work has enormous potential for increasing our understanding of why the sexes think the way they do.

From the evidence at hand it seems clear that a good part of the difference in intellectual functioning of the sexes has its beginnings in biology—in the different chromosomal inheritances of men and women, in differences in the lateralization of function in the two halves of the brain, and in the influence of hormones on brain structure. Without downgrading the part played by social conditioning, we are obliged to make room in our thinking for the existence of innate differences in the brains of men and women.

But what about the different achievement levels of men on the whole and women on the whole? In recent years we have all heard convincing arguments that men have generally been in charge and have prevented women from reaching positions of eminence and prestige. Many obstacles surely did exist; since World War II we have seen them being demolished one by one.

But what we have learned about the sexual dimorphism of the human brain suggests strongly that women will never be as numerous as men in engineering, architecture, and most of the physical sciences. The same argument turned around, however, suggests that women should be pre-eminent in activities depending on verbal fluency, such as literature and politics. It is true that women are well represented in these fields, but not to the point of challenging male dominance.

Even after obstacles have been removed and even in fields of their own choosing, women do not seem as aggressive as men in pursuing their goals. (In experimental psychology, aggressiveness is defined as behavior in which an animal approaches a stimulus instead of fleeing from it. This is roughly comparable to assertiveness in humans.) The study that is used by Maccoby, Hutt, and others to show this difference—it was done in 1956 and is therefore somewhat outdated—is a report on the academic careers of four hundred Radcliffe graduates who went on to earn Ph.D.'s and enter academic careers. These women professors were found to have published substantially fewer books and scholarly papers than their male colleagues. In fact, half of them had published little or nothing at all since earning their advanced degree.

Did the distractions of marriage and child care have a bearing on this low intellectual productivity? Apparently not, for there was no discernible difference between the married and the unmarried women. As Maccoby notes, the performance of the unmarried professors is the real puzzle, for "these women who are as well off as men (or perhaps better off) with respect to alternative demands on their time are nevertheless less productive."

Granting that many changes have occurred in the social climate since the Radcliffe study was made, Maccoby believes that a difference still exists—that women professionals pursue their intellectual careers less assertively than do men. Anyway, social conditioning is suspect as the entire explanation, since there are reasons for thinking that biology is at work here, too.

Aggressiveness is a biologically determined trait that is found more often in men than in women. Evidence of male aggressiveness comes from anthropologists, ethologists, and endocrinologists. It appears in virtually all human societies. The evidence of male aggressiveness in other mammals and in birds argues that it is not a characteristic of human society alone but a natural attribute of maleness. Finally, from studies with laboratory animals—rats, monkeys, and others—comes direct evidence that aggressiveness is influenced by the level of male hormones; that is, increased androgens result in increased aggressiveness.

Clearly, insofar as aggressive behavior is a desirable trait, the male animal has a considerable edge over the female, whether he is a white rat or a professor of the social sciences. And, as we have just seen, the hormones that control aggressiveness are also associated with levels of intelligence (or at least with high IQs). We are only beginning to make out the intricate patterns that are being woven by these influences on human behavior.

What are the principal implications of all this work? The female researchers themselves are in a unique position to tell us. Sandra Witelson believes that the differences between boys and girls in specialization of the brain's hemispheres may be critical when children are learning to read, and suggests that

different methods of teaching reading may have to be adopted for boys and girls. The warfare between advocates of the "look-say" method and the phonetic method may have obscured the fact that one method may be better with boys and the other with girls.

Speaking to a scientific meeting in Paris in the fall of 1976, Eleanor Maccoby urged that no doors of opportunity be closed on the basis of findings about the different intellectual constitutions of the two sexes. "There is nothing we know about the psychological predisposition of the two sexes that would place any constraints on the ways in which women can adapt to their new opportunities," she said. "So far women have proved themselves capable of undertaking successfully a remarkable range of extrafamilial activities. The only way to be sure about what further modifications of male and female roles are viable is to try them out."

Doreen Kimura believes that biologically determined differences arose as adaptations during the evolutionary process. Corinne Hutt pursues the same theme in describing her own contribution: "There can be little doubt that these sex-typical patterns of abilities and

behaviors are adaptive and, in evolutionary terms, have conferred distinct advantages. . . . To say this is not to discount the role of experience or learning, but it is as well for us to remember that experience acts on structure and machinery which is already biased to function in one particular direction. . . . Cultures and societies cannot create differences—they can only reflect and modulate those which already exist."

Now that it has been shown that there are sexual differences in what the genes transmit, in the hemispheres of the brain, and in the effects of hormones on the brain, we must also emphasize that these are average differences; they are of no use at all in predicting what a particular woman may accomplish in any field of activity. We accept this readily enough in the case of men and do not try to discourage young men from entering occupations in which female traits such as verbal fluency or persevering thinking are at a premium. Similarly, our new discoveries offer no argument at all for discouraging young women from becoming engineers or philosophers. ☐

Kenneth Lamott is a novelist and journalist with a special interest in the sciences.

The Nobel Experience

For six days at Stockholm the world
got a glimpse of America's
intellectual and scientific talent

Even the protester wore a white tie.

The climax is reached as, one by one, the laurea

Normally the physicist Burton Richter, who tracks down the basic form of matter, does not believe in fairy tales. But he concedes that for an unreal week last December he was part of one. "There were kings and queens," he recalls, "princes and princesses, chauffeur-driven limousines, and all the rest." The rest included instant recognition and adulation, feasts and toasts of aquavit that seemed to blend the long Scandinavian nights and the brief days into a ceaseless revel.

The Nobel Prize ceremony in Stockholm is the ultimate worldly reward for all those grinding, isolated years of intense intellectual labor. "When the trumpets sound," observed Saul Bellow, "you stop feeling skeptical." Since 1901, when a fund was established as designated by Sir Alfred Nobel in his will, the prizes have been awarded to those who are judged to have "conferred the greatest benefit on mankind." An award of $160,000 (shared when there are two recipients) is given each year to winners in six fields: physics, chemistry, medicine, literature, economics, and peace.

Adding to the enchantment of the most recent Nobel week was the fact that Americans took all five prizes (in a year of relative global calm, no peace prize was given out). Richter, a breezily cheerful scientist from Stanford University, who is forty-six years old, and Samuel C. C. Ting, a self-effacing forty-one-year-old Chinese-American from the Massachusetts Institute of Technology, shared the physics prize. The chemistry award went to William N. Lipscomb, Jr., a lean, raw-boned man who looks as if he would be more at home on the

By EDWIN WARNER

nd amid dignitaries and friends to receive the coveted Nobel medal.

range than in a lab. He is fifty-seven, a bona fide Kentucky colonel with an affidavit to prove it.

The medicine prize was divided between two researchers, both in their early fifties, who began their investigations in jungles far from America. Baruch Blumberg is a hearty, outgoing civic booster whose affection for Philadelphia is enthusiastically reciprocated. When the prize was announced, neighbors dropped by with cakes, bottles of Scotch, and cases of beer. Blumberg thought of the prize as a victory for his

home town. "It makes up for the Phillies not making it to the World Series," he said. D. Carleton Gajdusek, the other medicine winner, converses fluently in six languages, but he is most at home in the bush. When he was living in the eastern highlands of New Guinea, it occurred to him that civilized people in Paris, London, or New York considered the natives to be "remote museum pieces or subjects for arty films and literature. To me they are among the warmest and closest friends I have had."

Milton Friedman, who won the eco-

nomics prize, more than makes up for his slight stature (five feet three inches) with intellectual prowess. A conservative, he was, characteristically, campaigning for a proposition to limit state spending in Michigan when he learned of his award. He inspires an unusual animosity among leftists—which was manifested in Stockholm by constant demonstrations. The literature award, usually the most publicized, went to Saul Bellow, whose novels capture the rhythms of urban life and deftly characterize the deracinated intellectual.

47

Queen Silvia and an amateur photographer, Samuel Ting's daughter Jeanne

For all their marked differences of talent and temperament, the winners have some experiences and traits in common. No less than three—Blumberg, Friedman, and Richter—were born in Brooklyn, and a certain Flatbush flavor still lingers in their speech. In fact, Blumberg and Richter attended the same high school—Far Rockaway. One of the laureates, Bellow, was born in Canada; another, Ting, spent his youth in China. All are community-minded citizens who also have a variety of sports and musical interests—even passions. All are married family men with the exception of Gajdusek, who, while unmarried, has the largest family.

Though he has not kept strict count, Gajdusek has brought at least sixteen boys from New Guinea and other parts of Micronesia to his home in Chevy Chase, Maryland. There, amid native art, including a totem pole in the living room, he has raised and tutored them, sending seven of them through college. Fittingly, eight of his sons accompanied Gajdusek to Stockholm. Gajdusek feels that the best thing he can do for his boys is give them a good start in the modern world. He wryly speculated: "One of them, say, might become the dean of Columbia Medical School and use a little graft to put his relatives on the staff. Or he might become a U.S. admiral and set up a Mafia-like group to bring in his friends—the same tactics other ethnic groups use."

The winners do not take undue pride

in the American sweep; they tend, in fact, to play it down. Theirs are disciplines, they are careful to remind people, that transcend national boundaries. "Every writer knows there's no such thing as the American writer," says Bellow. "Dostoevski was as important in my life as Walt Whitman." The scientists point out that their prizes were based on discoveries of the past, when scientific research was generously funded by the U.S. government. They are critical of the fact that now, when it is still urgently needed, federal assistance for pure scientific research has been drastically reduced.

The American press did not go overboard on the prizes, for, as usual, triumph gets much less space than tragedy. However, the Nobel board was less reluctant to give America a pat on the back. In a speech that opened the week's festivities, the chairman of the board, Sune Bergstrom, after denying that the

A peek from backstairs at the banqueters

awards were an attempt to honor America in the year of its Bicentennial (the timing, he assured the audience, was purely coincidental), congratulated both the "unprecedented expansion" of research in the United States and also the "openness" of American society. As he put it, talented exiles from Europe were welcomed with open arms and pocketbooks. On American campuses professors and students cooperated easily in a "democracy of research workers." Nowhere else were promising young scientists given such an opportunity to embark on important projects early in their careers.*

The week's festivities definitely had an American accent. For one thing, so many Americans came along—family, friends, friends of friends, secretaries, home-town reporters, and hangers-on whom nobody could quite remember inviting. Blumberg apparently wanted to bring all of Philadelphia but had to settle for a mere twenty-eight. His secretary, Ann Dortort, who kept a sparkling diary of the week, noted that her party was "subtly but constantly reminded that we were the largest group ever to accompany a laureate. Not that it matters, they say. I wouldn't be surprised, though, if next year there was a limit."

The Americans were expected to play their part in the week's extended ritual, and for the most part it went without a hitch. Friedman explained: "If you take our World Series, plus the Superbowl, plus the presidential election and combine them into one, you have a remote idea of the importance of the ceremonies to Sweden." Gajdusek was astonished at the amount of work that went into selecting the prize winners. "If I had a chance to serve on that committee, I'd take it," he says. "It's the best job in the world. They talk better about my field than I can."

The climactic occasion was the award ceremony, when the laureates strode onto the radiantly lit stage of the concert hall into the presence of the king

*Since 1901 the United States has won more Nobel Prizes than any other nation: 126, of which 103 are in the fields of physics, chemistry, and medicine; in second place—Great Britain, 72.

Generous bouquets for the head table and gourmet fare for all twelve hundred guests

Baruch Blumberg, co-winner in medicine, with his wife, Jean, and their children before the royal palace

and queen, innumerable dignitaries, and, not least, the imposing bust of Alfred Nobel, who had made it all possible. American individuality triumphed over sartorial conformity, although white tie and tails were de rigueur. As Ann Dortort described them: "They looked impressive if not all quite alike. Some elastic underpinning showed, a missing cummerbund here, a protruding belly there. Yet by and large, the 'penguins' strutted into the lobby proud of themselves and even prouder of their beautifully dressed ladies."

Each laureate was introduced with a trumpet fanfare. His accomplishments were briefly summarized and he was presented with a gold medal. Then he bowed to the audience, right, left, and center, and returned to his velvet seat to sustained applause. Only Friedman's reception varied from the script, for as he was announced, a young man in the audience jumped up, blowing a whistle and shouting: "Long live the Chilean people! Friedman go home!" It was an allusion to the six days that the economist had spent in Chile in 1975 giving the right-wing regime the same kind of advice he gives everywhere: Get inflation under control.

Friedman showed no sign of being rattled. He took comfort from the fact that some people cuffed the protester as he was dragged out. The audience, Friedman felt, was with him. "If you had a tape of the ceremony," he insists, "you would discover that the ovation I received lasted longer than that of anybody else." For Blumberg, the outburst was a little touch of America—at least America as it was in the 1960's. "It reminded me of home."

The award ceremony was followed by a sumptuous banquet in the town hall. "It was like the invasion of Normandy," recalls Blumberg. There was such a crowd—some twelve hundred people—that every diner was given a map to find his seat. After dinner, there was dancing. In keeping with his conservative views, Friedman relished the "good old-fashioned waltzes and fox trots." They were not so relished by some of the laureates' kids who prefer rock. "My children didn't know how to do the traditional dances," said Richter, "so Elizabeth had to learn instantly."

Later on, the trumpets blared once again, this time to announce the arrival of mountainous trays of pastries, each crowned with a big *N*. When dessert was eaten, the trumpets announced the time for toasts, and the laureates rose to the occasion with lighthearted, self-deprecating remarks.

Friedman said: "As some of you may know, my monetary studies have led me to the conclusion that central banks could profitably be replaced by computers geared to provide a steady rate of growth in the quantity of money. Fortunately for me personally, and for a select group of fellow economists, that conclusion has had no practical impact, or else there would have been no central bank of Sweden to have established the award I am honored to receive. Should I draw the moral that sometimes to fail is to succeed? Whether I do or not, I suspect some economists may."

Bellow followed: "When I am praised on all sides, I worry a bit. I remember the scriptural warning: 'Woe unto you when all men shall speak well of you.' Universal agreement seems to open the door to dismissal. We know how often our contemporaries are mistaken. They are not invariably wrong, but it is not at all a bad idea to remember that they can't confer immortality on you. Immortality—a chilling thought. I feel that I have scarcely begun to master my trade."

There was a superabundance of food during the Nobel week. Still, some

Medicine laureate D. Carleton Gajdusek and eight of his adopted sons, with sleeping bags, at the Grand Hotel

American tastes were hard to satisfy. Sated on herring and reindeer meat, Matthew Richter longed for a hamburger. Since nothing is denied a Nobel laureate or his children, Matthew and Elizabeth were driven in a Mercedes limousine to a McDonald's, which fortunately does not serve reindeerburgers. The kids gorged. The limo got to be a habit; another evening, they went for a pizza and a movie.

December 13, Saint Lucia Day, began the earliest for the laureates. Around seven o'clock, each of them was awakened in turn by a vision of Nordic loveliness. Saint Lucia, a willowy blonde with seven candles flickering in a crown on her head, arrived at the hotel room door bringing light and a tray of coffee and pastries. The laureates had been alerted to this traditional ceremony and had prepared accordingly. Physicist Ting even arose two hours ahead of time to make sure he would not be surprised in the nude by the importunate saint. Judging from photographs, Bellow and his wife, Alexandria, were caught precisely in that state when the flaming maiden arrived.

This day turned out to be the longest for the revelers. They finally got a chance to let down their hair at a dance thrown by Swedish medical students. A group called the Swingin' Dentists played raucous rock nearly all night. "That was a high point of the trip," notes Blumberg, who seemed to enjoy more Nobel highs than any of the other laureates. Yet even his ample resources were taxed to the limit when the beauteous Saint Lucia put in another appearance. It is traditional for the medical laureates to carry her off at the end of the evening. Recalls Blumberg: "I tell you, she was one big girl, about six feet tall. They should be careful in the future to match up winners and Lucias, because if they get some little guy and a big Lucia, it could be disastrous. It took both me and Carleton to carry her. It was lucky there were two winners of the medical prize this year." As they struggled with their comely burden, Gajdusek remembers Blumberg muttering: "A Swedish Brunhilde." It was not until 5:30 A.M. that Blumberg called it quits. He had achieved another first. "They told me I stayed longer than any prize winner ever."

The final night was celebrated with a dinner at the royal palace attended by Swedish scientists and politicians. "It was like something out of the eighteenth century," says Blumberg. Later, over cigars and brandy in the Sun Room, the laureates and their families approached the royal couple in groups of four. "There was nothing stuffy about it," says Blumberg, who chatted with His Highness about their one mutual acquaintance: Mayor of Philadelphia Frank Rizzo, whom the king had met during a Bicentennial visit to the City of Brotherly Love. Richter reports that his son Matthew "developed a crush on the queen—a very charming young lady. I think he even promised to make her a skateboard. We'll see if he does."

The Nobel week had not been all fun and games. "We were given the red carpet," says Bellow, "but it was strewn with tacks." He meant the pointed questions of reporters who never stopped interviewing the laureates. "They wanted the blood from my veins," says Bellow, "the nails from my toes, the eyes from my scalp. Anyone treated like a beast soon gets a zoo look. I think the laureates should have been given a little more protection." Friedman, on the other hand, felt that he had too much of that. Bodyguards constantly accompanied him as he moved, meeting one hostile demonstration after another. "It was an unusual phenomenon," mused

51

BOTH:WIDE WORLD

Burton Richter, co-winner in physics, shares the glory with his team at Stanford.

the economist. "I felt like Henry Kissinger." He admits the protests detracted from the occasion but did not spoil it. He fought back in his customary feisty style. "Freedom of speech," he lectured protesting students, "must be accompanied by freedom to listen. Freedom of speech does not mean freedom to use force or coercion to prevent people from speaking."

The careers and pastimes of the laureates testify to the remarkable variety of achievement in American life, yet underlying the work of each is a common theme: a search for essentials. Both Blumberg and Gajdusek, for instance, seek the root causes of disease. Blumberg, who first studied infectious diseases in the swamp country of Surinam, says, "Everything is bigger and more dramatic there: bugs, plants, trees. The manifestations and effects of disease are much more dramatic, too, and easier to study." It was in such a setting in Australia in 1963 that Blumberg discovered an antigen, in the blood of an aborigine, that is part of the virus that causes hepatitis B. About 10 per cent of the population in the Far East carries the antigen; Europeans and Americans rarely do unless they are sick. His finding has made it possible to screen out many blood donors who are carrying the disease, and a vaccine that he and his colleagues developed for hepatitis B is now being tested.

The disease that Gajdusek found in New Guinea was repellent, but vital to the study of a kind of "slow virus" that assails the human nervous system. Kuru —meaning "shivering"—was the name and an accurate description of the ailment, which left its victims, usually women and children, laughing grotesquely and flailing uncontrollably until they inevitably died. The natives of the New Guinea tribe that had been decimated by the disease thought that they understood its origin. It was, they said, a form of masculine witchcraft: when a woman spurned a man's sexual advances, he took revenge by putting the spell of kuru on her.

To further his investigation, Gajdusek needed to examine the corpses of those killed by kuru—a somewhat difficult matter since the cannibalistic tribesmen made a practice of eating the victim's brains. For a long time he could find no cause for the disease. Finally, acting on a tip from a scientist who had studied a similar disease in sheep, he in-

jected chimpanzees with brain matter from the tribal victims. Several months later, the chimps showed symptoms of kuru. Apparently, when the natives prepared the brains of the dead, the infection entered their bloodstream— when they scratched an open sore or mosquito bite.

Once the tribe was encouraged to give up cannibalism, the disease disappeared. Now Gajdusek and his colleagues at the National Institutes of Health are convinced that the "slow virus" involved in kuru may be responsible for diseases in civilized countries, such as multiple sclerosis and Parkinson's disease. A common characteristic of these afflictions is rapid, premature aging. "Is old age perhaps such an infection?" muses Gajdusek. "Perhaps we are holding in our hands the key to the Fountain of Youth."

Seeking the essentials of matter itself, Richter and Ting, the physics winners, made the same vital discovery at virtually the same time. Yet neither man knew the other had done so. Richter, in fact, planned to spring his surprise on Ting, who visited him at Stanford in November, 1972. "Sam, I have some very exciting physics to tell you," announced Richter, to which Ting replied: "Burt, I have some very exciting physics to tell you."

Groups working under the direction of both scientists had achieved the isolation of a new subatomic particle, a basic building block of matter. The Ting

Students and friends celebrate at Harvard with chemistry laureate William Lipscomb.

group called the particle J because that letter resembles the Chinese character for Ting. The Richter forces dubbed it psi, the last remaining letter of the Greek alphabet that has not been given to a particle. By either name, the discovery was another landmark in the painstaking efforts to assemble a comprehensive theory of matter.

Richter and Ting may have reached their major discoveries by the same route, but they had widely differing upbringings. By the time he was a junior in high school, Richter knew he wanted to be a scientist. "I wanted to know how things worked," he recalls succinctly. He received his B.S. and Ph.D. degrees from MIT, and has been at Stanford for twenty years. He is a man who inspires trust among his colleagues. Notes one: "He has a way of asking you to do something so you can't say no. But you know darn well you better do it right and finish it on time."

Ting, on the other hand, reached his career pinnacle by a roundabout route. He was born in Ann Arbor, Michigan, where his father—a Chinese national—was attending the university. The family returned to China just in time for the Japanese invasion; until they moved to Taiwan in 1948, Ting never went to school—not that it has seemed to matter. At twenty, he decided to go back to America. "In China," he says, "I read that many Americans go through college on their own resources. So I informed my parents that I would do likewise." He arrived at Ann Arbor with only one hundred dollars in his pocket and no knowledge of English, but six years later, he had earned both his B.S. and Ph.D. at the University of Michigan. After stints at CERN, the nuclear laboratory near Geneva, and at Columbia University, in 1967 he went to MIT. It was there that he began the atom-smashing experiments that led to his Nobel Prize.

When Ting announced his discovery of the J particle, he simply presented the data, without offering a theoretical explanation for the evidence. It is his conviction that interpretations come

Samuel Ting (front) and co-workers commemorate the discovery of the J particle.

and go; only the evidence abides. He tries to get this point across to students, especially those from Third World countries. "When they come to the U.S.," he complains, "they immediately like to do theoretical work, and they feel it's somehow below their dignity to use their hands."

Like Richter and Ting, the chemistry winner, Lipscomb, has spent years in pursuit of the basic stuff of matter. No Kentucky marksman has stalked his prey more diligently than Lipscomb, hunting down the elusive structure of the borane molecule. Using complicated x-ray techniques, he discovered that the three atoms comprising the molecule were joined or "bonded" by only two electrons; until then, it was thought that two electrons could bond only two atoms. The discovery has clarified much that was mysterious in molecular behavior and has led to practical application in cancer therapy.

Lipscomb was born in Cleveland, but his family moved to Kentucky when he

was one; and in spirit he has never left the Bluegrass Country. He earned his B.S. from the University of Kentucky, and his Ph.D. at the California Institute of Technology. Since 1959, he has taught at Harvard. A skilled clarinetist, he likes to play chamber music with his two children—both aspiring scientists. Lipscomb is less proficient though equally dogged at tennis. On winning the Nobel, he received a letter from a biologist advising him how to spend the money: "Quick calculations show that you have funds for fifty thousand cans of tennis balls or two thousand tennis rackets or seventy-five silver flutes." Lipscomb does indeed plan to buy one tennis racket.

One hazard in Lipscomb's line of work is that when a tube of borane cracks, it is liable to explode. To prevent that, Lipscomb or his son pops the tube with a BB gun. Recently he received a letter from an elderly woman who had once been his baby sitter: "When you were a small child," she wrote, "I recog-

Awakened by a knock on his door, economist Milton Friedman meets Saint Lucia.

nized your intelligence, your creativity (if almost blowing up the house and other such antics could qualify) and your potential. The only thing that is a surprise about your winning the Nobel Prize is that you ever grew up to receive it."

Although Blumberg, Gajdusek, Richter, Ting, and Lipscomb—as scientists —are expected to search for essentials, such a concern for basics represents a departure from prevailing practice in the fields of economics and literature.

Milton Friedman, now sixty-four, has been preaching the basics of laissez-faire capitalism for years. His theories are based on the proposition that the marketplace is best equipped to manage the economy; tinkering and experimentation by government, including politicians and economists, usually makes things worse. The most important element in the economy, at least in the short run, is the money supply. Keep it growing at a modest, steady rate of 3 to 5 per cent a year, argues Friedman, and the economy will largely take care of itself. Such views have not endeared him to the dominant liberals in his profession. Admirers think that his conservative stance, along with such political activity as advising Barry Goldwater in his 1964 presidential campaign, kept Friedman from winning the Nobel Prize many years earlier.

The son of an immigrant dry goods merchant, Friedman worked his way through Rutgers University and went on to the University of Chicago, where he became the leader of the so-called Chicago school of economists, who warned that too much government involvement in the economy would contribute to runaway inflation. Now that that has proved to be the case in almost every nation in the Western world—not to mention the non-Western—Friedman is taken more seriously. Ultimately it was the climate of opinion that changed, not Friedman's opinion. The world came around to him.

If the winner in literature is from a major country, his presence usually sets the tone for the entire Nobel occasion. This was doubly true in Stockholm, where Saul Bellow, the diffident novelist from the Midwest, pleaded with writers to return to basic human themes. American writers especially have drifted from the "main human enterprise" into peripheral concerns, Bellow noted, while recalling his debt to Joseph Conrad, whose "themes were straightforward—fidelity, command, the traditions of the sea, hierarchy, the fragile rules sailors follow when they are struck by a typhoon." Analysts of American society are constantly making "extravagant, lurid, or demented statements" about the American condition, Bellow said. "These

analysts are produced by the very disorder and confusion they prescribe for. . . . The pictures they offer no more resemble us than we resemble the reconstructed reptiles and other monsters in a museum of paleontology." American readers need a "blessed and necessary release" from such formulations. Writers today may find it more difficult to reach the "whirling mind of a modern reader, but it is possible to cut through the noise and reach the quiet zone. In the quiet zone, we may find that he is devoutly waiting for us."

Bellow's eight novels (among them: *Humboldt's Gift, Mr. Sammler's Planet, Herzog*), his short stories, and occasional essays all reflect a quest for this quiet zone. Perhaps no other modern writer has a better ear for the harsh cacophony of urban life, and for the gentler harmonies that lie beyond. Bellow is street savvy, to be sure, but earth wise. Mortality clings to his characters whatever their intellectual pretensions. Bellow's books, in fact, are inventories of the intellectual bric-a-brac of our time, and by the end of each novel the bric-a-brac is pretty much swept away. "Shorter explanations, please," insists Mr. Sammler, who tries to bring the intellectual acrobats of Manhattan's upper West Side back to earth.

Bellow is heartened by the many letters he receives from people living outside the major metropolitan centers. "They are college-educated housewives," he says, "high school teachers, lab technicians, small-town readers who go to the public library, take out books and think deeply about them. They understand very well what I am up to. They look to me for a kind of strength that I don't see in myself." Bellow hastens to add that these readers should not be considered a silent majority. "Some intellectuals take me to task for being the Nixon of literature. If I seem to appeal vaguely 'out there,' I'm denounced for it."

To write the way he wants, Bellow, now sixty-one years old, chooses to live in Chicago, where he teaches literature at the University of Chicago. With his fourth wife, Alexandria, he leads a life of near anonymity, and that is the way he likes it. Writers such as Norman Mailer or Truman Capote may prefer to "play a Byronic role in the city, cut a figure in it. I'm not that sort of person. I don't need that kind of stimulus." Bellow particularly shuns New York because its "irritability, cynicism and vicious nervousness really put me off. If I were an intensely sadistic writer, I would feel deprived outside New York."

Bellow feels that American intellectual life has deteriorated alarmingly. "There is a difference between following the truth and striking postures," he says. Thoreau living at Walden Pond was at least physically outside the society he criticized. "Today, intellectuals are both comfortably within it and on prophetic occasions take a stand outside it. And this, if I may say so, is a bit corrupt." Intellectuals purport to "liberate the rubes and their middle-class brethren from bondage, from Puritanism, and lead them to creativity and self-discovery. This has resulted in a terrible confusion. Disorderly lives are accepted as natural and suitable."

Pleased as the Nobel winners are with their awards, they are also troubled. If the prize is the consummation of their careers, the aftermath is a time of testing. Richter believes that a laureate reacts in one of four ways. "There is the one who changes fields. Goes into something completely different. There's another who becomes a sage and makes pronouncements on all kinds of things. There's a third who does absolutely nothing. And there's a fourth who goes back to work. I hope I'm the fourth."

The prize has been particularly hard on writers, as Bellow is quick to point out. The burden of fame and public responsibility frequently drives an author not to write but to drink. Bellow acknowledged that the "child in me is delighted with the prize. But the adult in me is skeptical. Feelings of glory tend to remove you from the common fate, and it's not good for a writer to be removed from the common fate." Bellow feels that it is essential to recover his privacy.

Novelist Saul Bellow gets an admiring hug from his twelve-year-old son, Daniel.

"I'm much more interested in instruction than in glamour. The public feels you belong to them as a Nobel Prize winner. You owe them culture. They can be very indignant if you don't deliver."

He cites the example of a Chicago television broadcaster who was annoyed when Bellow complained about the ravenous press. Why then, the broadcaster wanted to know, did Bellow accept the prize? "I see it as a reward for merit," said Bellow. "They see it as a public service. That is simply nutty. It puts me in a situation in which no creative person can survive. There is no time to think or feel anything if you accept that public charge."

Alfred Nobel could not have expressed it better. The aim of the prize, after all, is to encourage work, not to stifle it. Considering the past obstacles that the laureates have overcome, there are grounds for optimism that they will surmount the Nobel Prize as well. That fairy tale in Stockholm was a beginning, not an end. □

Edwin Warner, who lives in New York City, is an associate editor of Time.

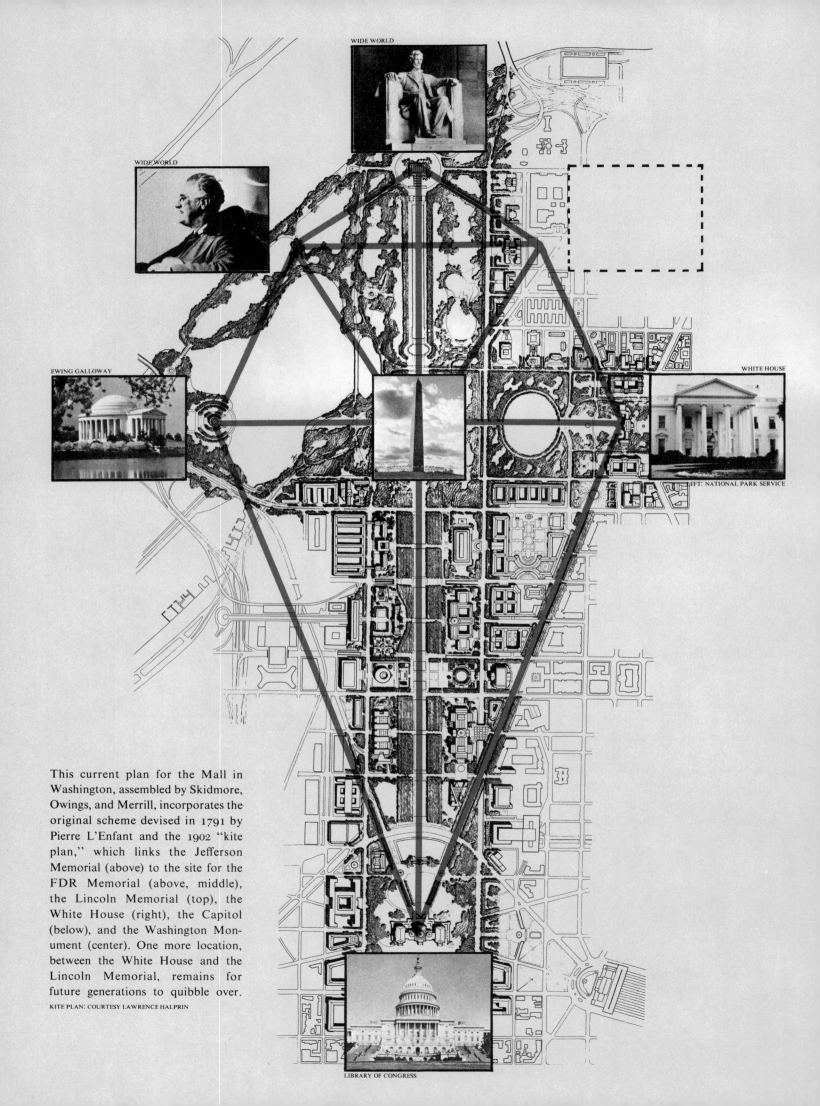

WIDE WORLD

WIDE WORLD

EWING GALLOWAY

WHITE HOUSE

LEFT: NATIONAL PARK SERVICE

This current plan for the Mall in Washington, assembled by Skidmore, Owings, and Merrill, incorporates the original scheme devised in 1791 by Pierre L'Enfant and the 1902 "kite plan," which links the Jefferson Memorial (above) to the site for the FDR Memorial (above, middle), the Lincoln Memorial (top), the White House (right), the Capitol (below), and the Washington Monument (center). One more location, between the White House and the Lincoln Memorial, remains for future generations to quibble over.

KITE PLAN: COURTESY LAWRENCE HALPRIN

LIBRARY OF CONGRESS

Washington, D.C., the city of imposing public monuments, may have a new memorial in a few years, though it will be neither imposing nor monumental. A park in honor of Franklin Delano Roosevelt has been designed by the West Coast landscape architect Lawrence Halprin and approved by the FDR Memorial Commission and the Fine Arts Commission. In June hearings will be held on its environmental impact before congressional funds are sought. The design's lack of grandiosity has led it to succeed where many others have failed.

At the moment, Roosevelt's memory is honored by a simple marker (at right, below) in front of the National Archives Building—the very thing in the very place he wanted. As he told Felix Frankfurter in 1941, he wished to have "a block about the size of this [putting his hand on his desk] . . . plain, without any ornamentation." But in 1955 Congress passed a resolution setting up the Franklin Delano Roosevelt Memorial Commission to make plans for a more elaborate monument.

A site was easily chosen, for the commission had the help of historic plans for the city, in particular the so-called kite plan for the Washington Mall, drawn up in 1902. One of the points of the kite (opposite) is in West Potomac Park, where cherry trees line the Tidal Basin. In 1959 this site was set aside for the FDR Memorial.

Settling on a design has been a frustrating, expensive, and occasionally comic process. In 1961, after a contest in which 574 entries were submitted, the commission chose the design (overleaf) of the New York architectural firm Pedersen and Tilney. Consisting of eight giant slabs, the largest 167 feet high and 65 feet across, it was quickly dubbed "instant Stonehenge" and failed to win the support of the Fine Arts Commission. Eventually Pedersen and Tilney scaled down the slabs and added a heroic statue of Roosevelt, but James Roosevelt, the president's son, opposed the original and the revised designs "unalterably." Both were shelved.

In 1966, taking a new tack, the memorial commission picked Marcel Breuer, designer of the UNESCO buildings in Paris and the Whitney Museum in New York, to submit a proposal. Breuer's design had seven rough granite "darts" (overleaf) radiating from a polished granite cube from which would issue recordings of presidential speeches (unfortunately reminding one of Roosevelt's grandsons of the "similarly amplified words of the Founder at Forest Lawn"). The Fine Arts Commission rejected the idea.

Back to the drawing board. In 1974 seven architectural firms were asked to submit suggestions, and Halprin's plan for an "experiential memorial"—one to be experienced—met with initial approval. Since then, Halprin has carefully detailed his design (pages 60 and 61), and if all goes well, Roosevelt may finally have a proper memorial, and Washington a tranquil and edifying park.

FDR and the Cherry Blossoms

After two false starts and much public controversy, Washington seems ready to memorialize a twentieth-century giant in proper relationship to his peers

Lawrence Halprin studies his scale model for the proposed FDR Memorial, which, if approved, is scheduled for construction in 1981. The existing Roosevelt monument, below, stands near the National Archives Building.

A Rogues' Gallery of Rejects

Both the Pedersen and Tilney and the Breuer designs below were approved by the FDR Memorial Commission but rejected after public outcries. The designs at right were all submitted for the original contest held by the commission in 1960. The commission had been reluctant to lay down guidelines for the competitors lest they "stultify the mind of the designer, perhaps paralyze him." Left to the simple instruction that "Roosevelt, the essential Roosevelt, must be the focus of an appropriate memorial," the would-be memorialists (identified at right) came up with a litter of pyramids (de Polo), a spacemobile out of science fiction (Barret), even a globe on what appears to be a giant slide carousel (Fagnani).

Harry Barret

Pedersen and Tilney

Minoru Yamasaki and Associates

Marcel Breuer

Leon N. Fagnani

58

Philip C. Johnson

Joseph D. Murphy and Eugene J. Mackey

Harry Rudolph de Polo

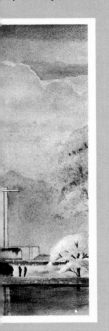

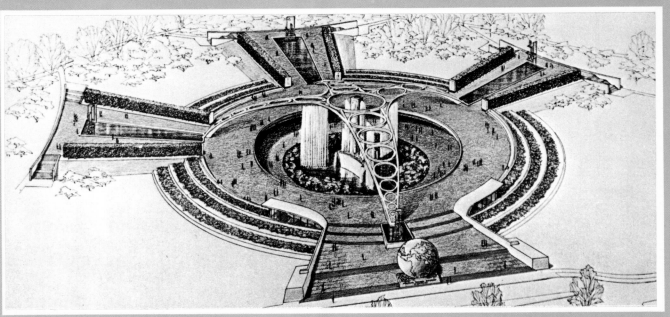

Faulkner, Faulkner and Associates

Davis, Brody and Wisniewski

Lorimer Rich

The Cherry Walk and the Jefferson Memorial

The water garden, from the architect's scale model

Details of the proposed garden wall, with bas-reliefs based on photographs of Roosevelt

N.S. section ....

FDR . Sections

conceptual sketch

Larry Halprin.

A sketch of the memorial, as seen from the Tidal Basin, with the water garden at left and the entrance at right

A Memorial for People

Lawrence Halprin describes his design for the FDR Memorial as "a place to visit for its own sake for personal enjoyment—as well as for its national significance. Therefore it should be serious not solemn." Just behind the Cherry Walk, opposite, he has planned a long sculptured garden wall that will be the major unifying element of the design. There will be four "rooms" created by indentations in the wall, places where visitors may stop to contemplate the bas-reliefs of Roosevelt and inscriptions of his most famous words.

Visitors will see the Washington Monument in the distance, below, as they approach the entrance plaza, which will have a clear view of the Lincoln and Jefferson memorials as well. Near the plaza, which marks one end of the fourteen-hundred-foot wall, a small theatre will present newsreels of the Roosevelt era. At the other end of the park will be a water garden—a playground of waterfalls, fountains, and pools that the memorial commission hopes will remind people of Roosevelt's love of swimming, sailing, and the U.S. Navy. More practically, the splashing will create a "white noise," screening the thundering of jets zooming in and out of National Airport. One of the best features of Halprin's scheme is that it will take up only seventeen acres, leaving undisturbed much of the recreational area of West Potomac Park.

An overview of the model, with the entrance plaza at top and the cherry trees left in place

The entrance walk to the memorial

Gymnastics Fever

Fired by dreams of Olympic stardom, thousands of kids—especially girls—are leaping, twisting, bouncing, and balancing in schools and gym clubs across the nation

Above: *Olympic stars Cathy Rigby (United States), Olga Korbut (Russia), and Nadia Comaneci (Romania) do their stuff.* **Opposite:** *A young Olympic hopeful is caught by her coach as she leaps down from the uneven parallel bars at the Diablo Gymnastics Club, Walnut Creek, California.*

"My dream and greatest hope is to be a gymnast. I watched Nadia, Olga, and many, many others, but Nadia is the one I always think of. I find myself to be very much like Nadia. Nadia was recognized and maybe I will be too. All I have to do is work at it. . . . I am longing desperately for a vault, a balance beam, uneven parallel bars, a coach, and competition. I signed up at the YWCA, but they said there were too many kids and I'm on a waiting list. I got very depressed. Could you send me a manual or something?"

Anne Cataffo, 14
Broadalbin, New York

Anne Cataffo's letter is just one of many such pleas received lately by the United States Gymnastics Federation in Tuc-son, Arizona, by former Olympic gymnasts Cathy Rigby Mason and Kim Chace, and by gymnastic coaches, sportswriters, and television commentators. American girls even write for advice to Olga Korbut in Russia and Nadia Comaneci in Romania. They say they want to be daring and dazzling like Olga, flawless and fearless like Nadia. And they are willing to work hard. The gymnastics fever has gripped the country, infecting not only youngsters but a number of adults, too. And for every new performer there are dozens of converted spectators. Gymnastics has become a spectacular and highly popular show. At the Montreal Olympics last summer Nadia Comaneci's room looked like a flower shop. "You have put joy into our lives," read one card sent by a couple from Chicago. It is the sort of accolade that is usually reserved for an opera star or a prima ballerina.

Unsmiling, her pale porcelain face somber with concentration, fourteen-year-old Nadia, five feet tall and with a wispy eighty-six-pound body, performed flawlessly and collected seven perfect scores of 10. No gymnast had ever before earned a single 10 in Olympic competition. And she won three gold medals, a silver, and a bronze. No matter that Nikolai Andrianov of Russia topped the world in the men's competi-

By ANITA VERSCHOTH

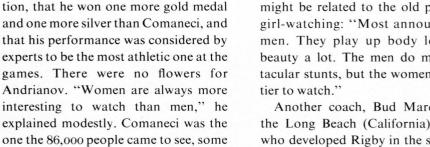

Outdoor training with coach Vannie Edwards at Olympia Manor, Belcher, Louisiana   *Classroom instruction, Poughkeepsie, New York*

tion, that he won one more gold medal and one more silver than Comaneci, and that his performance was considered by experts to be the most athletic one at the games. There were no flowers for Andrianov. "Women are always more interesting to watch than men," he explained modestly. Comaneci was the one the 86,000 people came to see, some of them paying two hundred dollars for a sixteen-dollar ticket. And millions more watched on television screens around the world.

Frank Bare, executive director of the U.S. Gymnastics Federation, does not understand how "little girls like Rigby, Korbut, and now Comaneci could cause this phenomenal boom in gymnastics, in *women's* gymnastics, in recent years. Maybe the explanation is that girls can see themselves engaging in an athletic activity that is both feminine and glamorous." But plenty of grown men and women, too, thrill to Comaneci doing her three back handsprings on the narrow balance beam. Abie Grossfeld, the men's gymnastics coach at Southern Connecticut State College in New Haven (his student Peter Kormann won the first Olympic medal, a bronze, for the United States in forty-four years at Montreal), thinks that Nadia's appeal

might be related to the old pastime of girl-watching: "Most announcers are men. They play up body looks and beauty a lot. The men do more spectacular stunts, but the women are prettier to watch."

Another coach, Bud Marquette, of the Long Beach (California) Turners, who developed Rigby in the sixties and early seventies, sees a change in the audience for gymnastics. "The public is better educated now. People realize that the girls are superb athletes, too. They see that gymnastics is as appealing and demanding as figure skating."

So girls who once would have trained at an ice rink and others who would have taken ballet lessons are now enrolling in gymnastics classes. Older women, too, have begun to work out in gyms to improve their bodies. Rhythmic gymnastics, a more balletic form of the sport that does not require apparatus, is even catching on in this country. Clubs have sprung up everywhere in recent years, and their members are mostly female and mostly young. As for the boys, some of them still think that gymnastics is a sport for sissies—an old and absurd stigma.

When blond and diminutive Cathy Rigby made the 1968 Olympic team at

the age of fifteen, the first flush of gymnastics fever became apparent. Her teammate, twenty-one-year-old Linda Metheny, was just as accomplished an athlete, but it was Cathy whom sportswriters singled out as "Pixie," "Kewpie doll," and "Barbie doll." Then, at the 1970 World Championships in Yugoslavia she won a silver medal on the balance beam—a first for an American girl. She cried when the medal was hung around her neck. Two years later, at the Munich Olympics, Korbut, the birdlike Russian sprite, wept bitterly when she fell off the uneven bars, and her audience cried with her. She also performed the first back flip on the beam and started the trend toward more athletic and acrobatic routines for girls. The drama Korbut acted out, deep despair in failure and boundless happiness when she triumphed the following day (she won three golds and a silver), started her romance with the public, which lasted four years. Then Comaneci took center stage, and if she is not loved quite as dearly as Korbut, she is revered for her perfection.

Gymnastics first came to the United States in the late nineteenth century, when immigrants from Germany and Czechoslovakia formed their Turner

BRUCE CURTIS

Olympic medalist and coach Muriel Grossfeld and one of her students, Milford, Connecticut

and Sokol clubs. (A German, Friedrich Ludwig Jahn, called the Old Man of gymnastics, had founded the first gymnastics club in Berlin in 1811.) But for decades the sport was thought to be something that people with heavy European accents did in the spirit of togetherness. Until 1962 it was only one of many sports governed by the Amateur Athletic Union, but the AAU did little for it. Gymnastics meets were badly organized; they often dragged on from two P.M. until two A.M., and two thousand spectators were considered a huge crowd. In 1960 there were about five thousand gymnasts in the whole country, a third of them girls, and only a few among them were active competitors. For the boys, the sport was part of the regular program in certain schools and colleges, but the girls had no other place to go but the few old Turner clubs.

Back in 1956, when Muriel Davis Grossfeld, now a successful coach in Milford, Connecticut (she is divorced from Abie Grossfeld), made the Olympic team at the age of fifteen, there were no more than two dozen serious women competitors to choose from. "We were just a handful," says Grossfeld, "but an amazing handful. We had no coaches, and we worked out on equipment that

can best be described as bizarre." By contrast, last year American girls had to pass through a seeding system of competitions on local, regional, and national levels before they could reach the Olympic trials, where twenty-six were chosen to compete for the team of seven that went to Montreal.

Frank Bare, an NCAA champion himself in the fifties, recalls those early days: "A typical championship meet would have forty-two men and eleven women, and we had a hard time putting together an Olympic team, which calls for six men and six women and two alternates. We took seven men to Tokyo in 1964, and though the seventh man

BRUCE ROBERTS—PHOTO RESEARCHERS

was injured and couldn't work, we still needed him as an alternate, because he was literally all we had."

In 1962 the top gymnastics coaches got together and decided to separate from the AAU and form the USGF. (It is a member of the International Gymnastics Federation, which sets the rules for international competitions.) Men's gymnastics was a part of the first Olympics of 1896—with individual competitions in the vault, the pommeled horse, the horizontal bar, the parallel bar, and the rings (floor exercise for men was added in 1956)—but women were included for the first time in 1928, and then only in team exhibitions. In 1952 they were finally allowed to compete in four events—the vault, the balance beam, the uneven parallel bars, and floor exercise.

The USGF enlivened the sport considerably. Many former competitors turned to coaching and opened private clubs. In Long Beach, Marquette started the Southern California Acro Team (SCATS) and was one of the first coaches to take girls, Rigby among them, to exhibitions in Europe. Now there were rewards for the hard work of training—travel, meeting people, and the large and enthusiastic European au-

Elementary gymnastics, Marietta, Georgia

65

diences. By 1970 there were about fifty thousand gymnasts in the United States, 75 per cent of them boys. Since then the USGF has had trouble keeping track of the numbers. "We figure there are now over half a million *competing* gymnasts in the country," says Bare, "and about eighty per cent of them are women."

A big club in the United States has four hundred students, most of them beginners, intermediates, or plain lovers of the sport. Only a dozen members are likely to get as far as one of the eight regional meets. From there those who post an average score of 9.0 compete in an elite qualifying meet, and the top fifteen there go on to the national championship. Elite students work out at their clubs six hours a day, six days a week, and usually pay a fee of $100 to $150 a month. In Connecticut, Muriel Grossfeld employs a staff of eight for her four hundred students (forty-five of them boys). She has recently opened a new $86,000 gym, and a second building is under construction.

According to Ed Knepper, the director of the U.S. Independent Club Association in Wilmington, Delaware, the number of clubs has risen to three thousand, many of them with three hundred to four hundred students and a half dozen coaches. Spectator figures have increased, too: crowds of fourteen thousand to eighteen thousand have become quite common for such drawing cards as the visiting teams from Russia or Romania, especially when Korbut or Comaneci is along. Even the very first Russian tour of the United States in 1973, with Korbut and company, which was underwritten by Fabergé, the cos-

Handstands, Ribbons, and Trampolines

When the Russian team toured eleven U.S. cities in 1976, the sports acrobats (right) and the modern rhythmic gymnasts (center) gave spectacular performances. Popular in the USSR for years, these balletic offshoots of gymnastics require no apparatus but demand exceptional strength and artistic skill. Acrobatics involves tumbling and hand balancing; rhythmic gymnastics combines a rope, hoop, ball, or ribbon with floor exercise. In recent years both variants of gymnastics have caught on here, and U.S. competitors are now training for international meets. Meanwhile, gymnastics demonstrations by American athletes (far right) continue to keep the public enthralled in arenas throughout the country.

metics company, drew huge crowds in eight cities and eventually earned its own way at the box office.

"Before Munich," says Marlene Bene, Bare's assistant, "you could not sell a gymnastics event to a big arena. Competitions were held at university gyms. Now we can get any big arena in the country. Madison Square Garden is always sold out. An exhibition by the Russians in Cleveland in 1975 attracted 20,202 people, our biggest crowd ever."

Television stations are clamoring not only for such exhibitions and competitions but also for prime-time specials like the CBS documentary "Nadia— From Romania with Love." Indeed, the money earned from television is filling the coffers of the USGF. According to Rick Appleman, who handles promotion for the USGF, "Our 1976/77 con-

tract with ABC provides us with ten times the revenue we received from TV in 1973." The federation's total budget has gone from $37,000 in 1963 to $560,000 last year.

Still, in international competitions U.S. gymnasts have been badly lagging behind the Eastern Europeans. At the Munich Olympics, Rigby finished tenth overall, and in Montreal Kim Chace was the top American girl, in fourteenth place. "We need to start girls at an earlier age on the difficult tricks," says Chace, who is now twenty-one and coaches at her father's school in Revere Beach, Florida. "I learned to do one twist. Now they are doing double twists in floor exercise. It takes years to build up enough strength and muscles so that you don't get hurt when you try these things."

How to do a twisting somersault vault, as demonstrated by Nadia Comaneci.

Although American girls are going into gymnastics at an earlier age—Muriel Grossfeld takes them at three and a half—many clubs are so concerned about the possibility of lawsuit if a student is injured that they are cautious about what they teach. "Instructors are leery of teaching difficult tricks," says Ed Knepper. "One gymnast gets hurt and the coach can have his entire livelihood wiped out. In Russia they don't sue."

"It's a problem," says Muriel Grossfeld, "but I have never been able to find a direct relationship between the level of gymnastics and the degree of injury. I have four girls doing double back somersaults, but they don't get injured. It's the kids who come once a week we have to watch out for especially."

Will a little American girl now ten years old be the Nadia of 1980 in Moscow? Not likely, as long as such countries as East Germany, Romania, and Russia, which have always been strong in gymnastics, enjoy the advantage of well-organized, efficient, and government-subsidized long-range programs. Comaneci was picked out by her coach, Bela Karolyi, from a kindergarten class when she was six. (In the past American girls did not even start gymnastics until they were thirteen.) She worked out at his government-sponsored school for seven years. Then, at the 1975 European championships in Norway, in her first senior competition, she was the surprise winner. Karolyi, who has been combing kindergartens since 1962, believes that a girl's career lasts from the age of eight until twenty. "During those years there is no fear," he says. "No problems.

Women gymnasts have done so many more difficult feats in recent years because they are younger now."

Knepper thinks there is one more big difference between our girls and the East Europeans. He insists that their chances of succeeding are enhanced by a greater desire to find a way out of a drab life. "Sports is all they have," he says. "Our country offers too many distractions." However, Rod Hill, who runs the Denver School of Gymnastics, points out that "some of our coaches push their kids too hard. If you do that, a kid will say, 'The heck with it,' and drop out."

Muriel Grossfeld thinks we have adequate facilities, "but we need better direction," she says. Sometimes described as a tough coach determined to produce Olympians, Grossfeld says that she hates "this violent push that everybody

Training is rigorous in Romania for these young girls tutored by Bela Karolyi, Nadia's coach.

has to become an Olympian. I just want to turn out the best gymnasts I can." But if one of her students shows up over-weight, Grossfeld is liable to ban her from the gym "until that situation has been corrected."

Former Olympian Linda Metheny, who runs a gymnastics academy at Eugene, Oregon, with her husband, Dick Mulvihill, says, "We have a few girls who are as dedicated as a Coma-neci. We have enough clubs and a lot of coaches, but we need more knowledge-able coaches. We lack in the area of research—the mechanical analysis of all the movements—and in the psycholog-ical aspects of the sport. The Romanians do training in areas of mental discipline and concentration. We coaches have got to get together. We have to start a national program to find out where the new talent is."

Thanks to the USGF's lucrative tele-vision deals, such a program is now get-ting under way. Last January, Bare asked coaches around the country to send their top juniors, girls aged ten to fourteen, to a special testing session at Springfield, Missouri, specifying certain requirements pertaining to body type, athletic style, commitment, and cour-age. Thirty-three girls showed up, and

they were put through a series of dif-ficult compulsory moves—"the kind of moves," said Dick Mulvihill, "that we felt would be required in 1980." The girls were also tested on their optional routines and were given a dance test, in which they could demonstrate flexibil-ity, strength, balance, their ability to jump, and their creativity in harmony with the music. Finally, they were exam-ined to see whether they were over-weight or had a tendency to become overweight.

The ten best performers at Springfield now make up a new Junior National Team Program, which will hold at least four training sessions a year, all ex-penses, including air fare, to be paid by the USGF. (The first of these sessions is being held this month in Eugene, Oregon.) The athletes will be introduced to the caliber of competition required at the Olympic level, and then they will be expected to work on the new skills back at home. Famous coaches, such as Bela Karolyi, will be invited to these sessions to help train the team. The USGF is planning a similar program for boys.

Whether the program is successful may become apparent at the 1978 World Championships in Strasbourg, France. "At least," says Bare, "we are no longer

assembling the team at the airport before we go to an important interna-tional competition. We've got a year and a half to get these youngsters ready." Vannie Edwards, a Belcher, Louisiana, coach who was appointed the program's national director, thinks that the choice made at Springfield was a good one: "These kids are exceptional; they need special treatment. If we want to hang in there with the rest of the world, we've got to motivate that exceptional child."

One of the exceptional ten is fourteen-year-old Leslie Pyfer, whose most dif-ficult trick at Springfield was a back flip on the beam with her legs held *straight* (which is quite a bit harder to do than the original Korbut flip). "I think this program is really neat," she said, flushed with enthusiasm. "I'll train real hard so I can make the team for the 1980 Olympics, and then I'll try to get a medal."

"Will you try to become as good as Nadia Comaneci?" she was asked.

"Better," she said, without batting an eyelash. □

Anita Verschoth covers gymnastics, as well as track and skiing, for Sports Illus-trated.

Day one at an American school

PRESENT INDICATIVE

Five Ws for the Counterculture

His name is Tom Robbins and to many he is the current maestro of the counterculture (literary division). A former newspaper reporter in his thirties, he retreated to the gentle wilds of northwest Washington State, styled himself a recluse, and wrote novels that have invaded dormitories across the land. His first, *Another Roadside Attraction*, sold over half a million copies; his second, *Even Cowgirls Get the Blues*, was well over 150,000 before it appeared in a mass-market paperback.

Another Roadside Attraction is a rambling hodgepodge of anecdotes, aphorisms, and riddles that makes no pretense to narrative style. *Cowgirls* does have a story line of sorts, tracing the adventures of Sissy Hankshaw, hitchhiker, and her friends, who include a feminine-hygiene-

Best-selling novelist Tom Robbins

deodorant mogul, an asthmatic Mohawk water colorist, and a group of joyously bisexual cowgirls. But the real fun of *Cowgirls* is its author-to-reader asides, its jazzlike riffs on the nature of life, and the singular way in which the novel talks to itself. "This sentence has accepted Jesus Christ as its personal savior. . . . This sentence can do the funky chicken. . . . This sentence is proud to be a part of the

team here at *Even Cowgirls Get the Blues*. . . . This sentence is rather confounded by the whole damn thing."

Confounded, too, are the critics, who alternately hail Robbins as brilliant or condemn him as self-indulgent, and who have compared him to everyone from Pynchon, Vonnegut, Brautigan, Nabokov, and Borges to (ridiculously) Joyce, Twain, and Homer. Undeterred and unrepentant, Robbins is working on his next book, tentatively called *Woodpecker Rising*. After all, he explains, his goal is merely to satisfy the famous five Ws, which journalists know as Who, What, When, Where, Why, but which Robbins defines as Wow, Whoopee, Wahoo, Why not, and Whew.

Fighting Street Dance

To overcome their fear of unknown assailants stalking city streets, many Americans have taken instruction in some form of Oriental self-defense. Karate and jujitsu are rivaled in popularity by taekwon-do, aikido, tai chi chuan, kung fu, and even the Burmese bando. But for those who are weary of the solemn intensity of the Oriental style, there is a merrier sort of martial protection available from Brazil called capoeira (pronounced ka-poh-air-ah).

Capoeira is so light and quick that its participants seem to be playing with each other. Often fighters will escape the flying kicks of opponents by slithering on the ground. So although it is as lethal as other methods of self-defense, capoeira is livelier and more entertaining. And, after all, entertainment and the desire to keep in shape are the civilized reasons for engaging in martial arts.

What may have once been a form of ritual combat in Angola, the practice eventually came to Brazil, where Portuguese planta-

A Brazilian in Brooklyn, Jelom Vieira (left), demonstrates the art of capoeira.

tion owners banned it to keep their slaves from fighting. In order to disguise its true aggressive nature, capoeira acquired the playful, acrobatic finesse that now characterizes it. And when urged on by cowbells, congas, and the shouts of onlookers, practitioners of capoeira tumble into a dance as exuberant as Brazilian Carnival antics. Today Brazilians consider it their second national sport (after soccer), and even the limber Pelé has taken lessons.

Performances in this country are rare, but interest in the all-purpose capoeira is gaining. Last year the Smithsonian Institution included demonstrations in one of its traveling exhibitions, and a capoeira academy has opened in New York City. For black and Hispanic Americans trying to trace their roots to Africa and

South America, capoeira is more than a spirited way to beat off muggers.

Alarm Belle

Nearly every cub photographer has his standard shot of a three-alarm fire. Jill Freedman did more than chase fire trucks to the scene of action. For her book of 135 photographs, *Firehouse*, published by Doubleday this month, she spent nearly half a year with three fire companies in New York City, often sleeping in the firehouse in the back seat of the fire chief's car because the dormitories were for men only. The result is an intimate portrait showing the courage, camaraderie, and humor of the group of men behind the news stories.

Particularly telling are the pictures taken after fires were put out: exhausted men, with faces blackened by smoke and erased of all expression, reflect each other's weariness. In others they sit around the firehouse, winding down after a late-night run, but ready for yet another.

Freedman's companies are in Harlem and the South Bronx, in some of the most devastated areas of the city, and her pictures show the warmth and respect for the firemen felt by the people in these neighborhoods, who normally do not trust men in uniform. She recalls one old woman in the South Bronx who, after the fire in her building had been put out and the residents calmed, said simply, "Thanks, firemen. There's a lot of children live here."

Never Pull Off Tomorrow

Harry Mathews is an American poet and novelist who likes to play word games. One of the simpler games is concocting the perverb, which joins the first part of one proverb to the last part of another ("Lucky at cards, but you can't make him drink"). Equally amusing are such "snips of the tongue" as "Half a loan is better than no bread," "Once burned, twice snide," and "Never pull off tomorrow what you can do today."

More complex structures are devised by the members of a group of experimental writers to which Mathews belongs in Paris. One of them has composed an entire novel using actual French words, but without the letter *e*. Another has written a set of ten sonnets, each line of which is interchangeable with its counterpart in the other nine sonnets. The result? Raymond Queneau's *One Hundred Thousand Billion Poems*, each line conveniently printed on a separate slip of paper so that the reader can put together the 10^{14} options available. Or, as Mathews might say, "The early bird leaves no term unstoned."

Chimney Stack, Upside-down

Though it took no carving, chiseling, or molding to make, Claes Oldenburg's latest creation will probably still be called sculpture by those who see it towering in the plaza of the Great Lakes Social Security Program Center in Chicago. The new work is a twenty-ton, see-through steel baseball bat called *Batcolumn*, and what did bring it into existence was months of welding by twelve visored workmen.

Resting on a four-foot-high pedestal, the bat—a twenty-seven-inch-high granite knob topped by a gray latticework column (see sketch, right)—is ten stories high, making it thirty times bigger than anything Ernie Banks ever pulled off the rack at Wrigley Field.

Oldenburg provided models and supervision, but *Batcolumn* was constructed at the Don Lippencott foundry, in North Haven, Connecticut. "With so many people contributing, it became a monumental effort of engineering as well as design, like the Eiffel Tower," said Donald Thalacker, director of the federal Art in Architecture program that commissioned the column.

Why a bat? The nonathletic Oldenburg, who grew up and first worked as a news reporter in Chicago, explains his fondness for the shape: "Chicago is full of fat chimney stacks which get narrower toward the top. I wanted to invert that to create a structure thin at the bottom and wider as it goes up."

What better structure, then, than a Louisville Slugger, similar to the other ordinary objects of modern life, such as electric plugs, typewriter erasers, and lipsticks, that Oldenburg has elevated to icon status?

A few surly fellows, including Senator William Proxmire of Wisconsin, have taken swings at *Batcolumn*'s $100,000 price tag, especially because it was met out of tax money. "But," says Thalacker, "that's a very reasonable fee for such an artist as Oldenburg, whose reputation is of heroic proportions." Not to mention his fabrications.

Three New York City firemen take a break after fighting a fire.

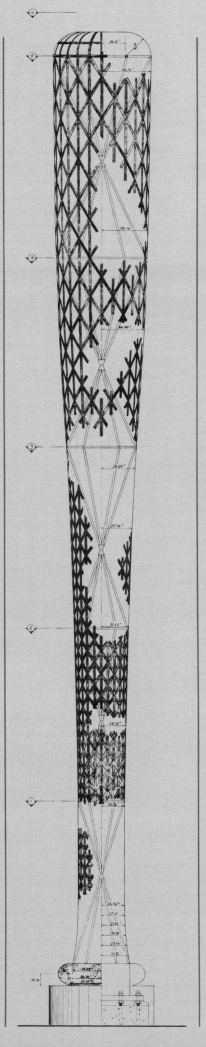

Bringing Bold Splendor to the City

Adding drama and grandeur to urban life, Henry Moore's sculptures adorn plazas, courtyards, squares—even traffic circles—the world over

"I think that the authorities, whoever they are, should look upon towns as though they are creating a house for the inhabitants to enjoy and to live in," Henry Moore said recently. Himself a major contributor to the enhancement of town and city life, he probably has more of his works in public places than any other sculptor in history.

These photographs of Moore sculptures are the work of David Finn, a friend and admirer of the artist who, during the past six years, has indefatigably tracked down Moore's pieces in Europe, the United States, Australia, and Japan. The result of his odyssey is a book of some 495 photographs, *Henry Moore: Sculpture and Environment* (published this month by Harry N. Abrams, Inc.), which Moore hopes will "show architects, government officials, and the general public that there are hundreds of public places well suited for the placement of sculpture."

If Moore's own artistry is taken as evidence, the right sculpture in the right place can be a dramatic focal point for urban space that might otherwise seem stark or bare. And in their vigor Moore's sculptures in the city testify to the vitality of urban life itself.

Jutting horizontally and vertically, The Archer *(1964–65) stands in the civic square of Toronto, a placement that Moore characterizes diffidently as "not a bad one." At left, the enormous bronze* Reclining Figure *(1963–65) lies resplendent in its reflecting pool at Lincoln Center in New York.*

In a large square on the outskirts of Prato, Italy, surrounded by an expanse of green lawn, is Square Form with Cut *(1969–70), which was carved from several layers of marble.* Upright Motive no. 8, *opposite, repeats the vertical thrust of the Chiyoda Insurance Company outside of Tokyo; Moore thinks that in this setting the sculpture appears Japanese, "like a pagoda on top."*

Nuclear Energy *(1964), which Moore says represents "man's cerebral activity" as well as the destructive element of the atom bomb, stands at the University of Chicago on the spot where the first controlled splitting of the atom took place. Below, set against graceful Parisian rooftops, is the marble* Reclining Figure *(1957–58) in the UNESCO complex; at right, the bronze* Warrior with Shield *(1953–54) lends an uncanny presence to the central square of Arnhem, in the Netherlands.*

Near the National Museum in West Berlin is another cast of The Archer; *when Finn saw it in this setting, he "almost thought it was a different work from the cast in Toronto." Standing proudly, like lords themselves, in front of the House of Lords in London, the towering bronze forms of* Knife Edge: Two Piece (1972), *opposite, echo the soaring grandeur of the Gothic architecture behind.*

The Fine Art of Collecting Photographs

Savvy and inexperienced collectors alike are entering the booming market for photographs. Here, for the would-be collector, is a basic guide to finding and buying everything from antique tintypes to prints by the great masters

Los Angeles, *by Grant Leighton Mudford*

Three Magrittes in One Image, *by Duane Michals*

Already prized by the experts, but still reasonably priced, is the work of these younger contemporary photographers.

Fashion photograph by Deborah Turbeville

In the early 1930's, the Metropolitan Museum of Art in New York bought three hundred photographs by Mathew Brady, the great Civil War photographer, for ten cents apiece. Today each one is worth at least several hundred dollars. Thirty years later, when one of the museum's staff members was going to England, he was given, as an afterthought, $150 to buy some photos by Julia Margaret Cameron, the nineteenth-century English pioneer photographer. The museum man got thirty Camerons for that amount. Now few of the great lady's images sell for less than $1,200.

In 1974 the American collector Sam Wagstaff made the winning bid of $120,000 at Sotheby's in London for an album containing ninety-four Cameron photographs that had been presented by her to Sir John Herschel, the noted nineteenth-century scientist. But the British Reviewing Committee on the Export of Works of Art withheld an export license for the album on the grounds that it was a national treasure—apparently the first time this had ever happened in England to anything photographic. Public donations, together with an appropriation from the National Art-Collection Fund and the help of private foundations, met the auction price, and the album is now safely housed at the National Portrait Gallery in London. Only a short time before, the gallery had acquired 258 Hill and Adamson photographs from the Royal Academy for $80,000. No one had asked to see them at the Royal Academy in more than one hundred years.

Today, photographs are steadily increasing in popularity and, therefore, in price. But the number of fine photographic prints are nowhere near as numerous as the public believes, and competition for certain key images has accelerated with astonishing results.

Take the six daguerreotypes bought for $20 in San Francisco several years ago. Authenticated by the Library of Congress as originals taken by John Plumbe in 1846, they were promptly

resold by the new owner for $12,000. A daguerreotype portrait of President Martin Van Buren, circa 1856, bought for $45 in a Pennsylvania antique shop, was resold for $6,000 shortly afterward. And there is the much-publicized tale of the 1848 daguerreotype of Edgar Allan Poe by an unknown photographer. It sold for $9,250 at a Chicago auction in 1973, was resold immediately for a reputed $18,000 to New York dealer Scott Elliott, and subsequently acquired —in a complicated deal—by collector Arnold Crane, back in the Windy City, for about $35,000!

The story of collecting photographs is clearly one of profits to be made by dealers and savvy collectors, but it is

An unknown photographer's daguerreotype of Edgar Allan Poe sold at auction in 1973 for $9,250—then a record price. In a subsequent acquisition it was priced at about $35,000.

also about the passion expended by photography lovers to get what they want.

• • •

In collecting photographs, as in any other creative endeavor, there's only one way to improve—practice. "It's a combination of mental perception and physical endurance," one energetic collector says. "You have to go out and look, look, look. But all the looking in the world isn't going to do you any good if you haven't any idea of what to look *for*, or what you are looking *at* once you're standing in front of it."

So where do you begin?

"You immerse yourself in books of

photographs," counsels Weston Naef, associate curator of prints and photographs at the Metropolitan Museum. "Before anyone buys his first print, he must know what the world of editors, publishers, scholars, and critics has defined as 'desirable pictures.' Considering that photography is an exceedingly ubiquitous medium with literally millions of pictures having been made and still being made each day, the key question becomes, 'How do I sort out from these millions of photographs those worth preserving?' "

In the last couple of years publishers have at last begun to produce more books of photography, both by the famous photographers and by the newcomers. Now one can sit down with titles ranging from *Sixty Years of Photography: 1912–1972* by André Kertész to Danny Lyon's *Conversations with the Dead*, a body of photographs dealing with prison life; from Brassaï's *Secret Paris of the Thirties*, a revelation of the French capital's morals of the time, to Judy Dater's and Jack Welpott's *Women and Other Visions*.

While many of the photo books are themselves collectible, especially those now out of print, their main value to a learner is to make him ask, "Which photographs do I like? Which don't I like?" These are the two easiest questions to wrestle with, according to Naef. "But it is the in-between images, those that trigger no response at all, which really deserve the inquisitive collector's attention," he says. If you don't agree with the editor's choice, then you must figure out why. The more mental grappling of this sort you do, the more defined your aesthetics will become.

Reading such basic texts as Beaumont Newhall's *History of Photography* as well as Helmut and Alison Gernsheim's *Concise History of Photography* is indispensable in establishing the foundation for any collector's own scholarship. But for more up-to-date information consider attending lectures on photography given in many museums as a way to familiarize yourself with key practitioners and their work.

By LANDT DENNIS AND LISL DENNIS

Adult education courses, symposiums financed by foundations and publications, summer photography workshops at universities and by groups of photographers—all enable collectors to learn and to hone their tastes.

"But there is nothing better than getting your hands wet in the chemicals themselves, learning the actual technicalities of the medium, the darkroom side of things, too," says Casey Allen, moderator of a television program called "In and Out of Focus." "You will never know what a truly fine photography print is unless you know what is required to make one. Only then can you, as a collector, judge the fine print skills of a photographer who is a masterful darkroom technician versus the mediocre print of a photographer who is not. Or who doesn't care." Since, as Ansel Adams says, "the negative is the score, the print is the performance," familiarity with the printing process cannot help but give a collector greater confidence when making a purchase.

Getting to meet and, perhaps, to know some of the photographers themselves adds another dimension to an aspiring collector's judgment. Leading photography centers frequently offer lecture series where such people as Inge Morath and Arnold Newman are willing to conduct a dialogue with an audience. The International Center of Photography in New York, now in its third year, attracts several hundred listeners per semester for the famous photographers who appear there.

The newcomer should go into photography collecting slowly, step by step, until the taste buds begin to be activated toward certain images and the work of certain photographers comes to demand particular attention. Then the collector can decide whether to collect works by people living today and in their prime or to delve into the past and have a collection that is more historic and that contains more undisputed big names.

Whether one is interested in photographs purely as an investment will play a part, of course. If so, vintage images will be one's main focus. But if

One-of-a-kind images, like this daguerreotype of an American couple, have soared in value.

potential financial rewards aren't of paramount importance, then one can study and buy mainly the work of young artists. However, as critic Gene Thornton warns, "Steady nerves and a strong conviction of the rightness of one's own judgment are needed to collect in the avant-garde area, for no one can ever be certain what part of today's avant-garde will be tomorrow's classic. . . . the rewards could be a pace-setting collection that could grow in value and esteem."

Photo galleries, both in large cities and small, in the United States and abroad, are multiplying faster than the yellow pages of the telephone book can list them. But they are more in evidence in New York City than anywhere else. In Manhattan at least thirty photography and private photography dealers, many of whom sell paintings and graphics, too, now offer collectors inventories to pore through. (Most are open Tuesdays through Saturdays, and only a few of the dealers require advance appointments.) The galleries vary enormously, however. Well-established galleries in prime urban areas inevitably have a Bigelow on the floor, a Weston to the front of you, an Adams to the rear, an Imogen Cunningham on the right, a Berenice Abbott on the left. Less-affluent galleries, frequently run by the photographers themselves, or even by a camera club, settle for hardwood floors, exposed plumbing, low rent, and very often some of the most progressive work going on in the field today. A look at the list of galleries in leading pho-

tography magazines or the Sunday art sections of newspapers will give the collector enough addresses to keep him busy for quite a while.

"It is extremely important to find a dealer in whom you have confidence," says the editor of a prominent arts magazine. "That is usually determined by their track record. Who they represent. Who their other customers are. Who they have 'discovered.' Normally it's also wise to deal with someone who has been in business at least five years. Of course, this is difficult with photography collecting so new. But the point is that you want to be sure they're still around in the future if you have a complaint.

"Most important of all, though, you must have rapport with dealers if you intend to do business with them regularly. They must be able to understand exactly what it is that you are looking for to build up your collection, and if they are to advise you, you must feel that their taste and judgment are astute." A gallery owner who likes you will sometimes let you see what he has for sale before he puts it on his walls. A good dealer will go out of his way to help out a collector he thinks is serious.

One of the mistakes many newcomers to photography make is that they "walk into a gallery for the first time, look at what's on the wall, then walk out," says Leslie Simitch of the Enjay Gallery in Boston. "They think they've seen everything, but it isn't so." Drawers of photographers' work are usually available to anyone who asks to see them.

Victor Schrager, director of the Light Gallery in New York, tells about a newcomer who "came in and went through absolutely every single image we had in stock. It took him four days. Finally he made up his mind and bought quite a few. The remarkable thing was he was only seventeen years old."

Another reason gallerygoing is important is the chance it offers to see a photographer's works that haven't been seen before. Shortly after he arrived in the United States, Grant Mudford, a young Australian photographer, got a Madison Avenue gallery show for his black-and-white pictures of galvanized steel fences, moving vans, and warehouses. The result was immediate and steady sales. "We liked his work and were willing to take a chance," the gallery director says. "But I admit we didn't think the public would react so favorably so quickly."

Auctions have also become prime sources of photographs for today's collector. Christie's and Sotheby's in London, Martin Gordon and Sotheby Parke Bernet in New York are some of the leading auction houses for photography. Out-of-town collectors can send for a catalogue and make their bids by mail. "It is always better to be there in person, though," cautions an experienced auctiongoer, "and to have seen the images at the exhibition beforehand. Your choice may not look as good 'in the flesh' as it did in catalogue reproduction. And a mail-order bid can lose out by twenty-five to fifty dollars to someone who's in the room at the time of the actual auction."

According to Anne Horton of Sotheby Parke Bernet, "Something rather ironic about photographs in catalogues is that people frequently say, 'Oh! It looked better on the page than it does now that I see the real thing.' What has happened is that people are now so used to printing's halftones that pure black and white throws them."

Used bookstores, flea markets, antique shops, anywhere graphics are sold will usually have photographs too. But nowadays the owners are apt to recognize their worth. Of course, you may find your photos in a family trunk and get them for free.

Here are some of the most collectible items currently catching attention:

(1) Postcards. Brightly colored old postcards are especially popular. They are often views of landmarks like Niagara Falls and the Eiffel Tower. Sam Wagstaff began collecting this way. "I even go through the postcard racks today at airports when I travel," he says. "Postcards relate to common taste, and in many ways that's what photography is all about."

(2) Stereograms. The source of an evening's entertainment in many American and European homes at the turn of the century, these double images are often buried beneath great-grandmother's wedding dress. Those that have come out of hiding are being increasingly sought by collectors and are rising in price. "I think [stereo views] are the greatest thing in photography, telling more effectively the history and sociology of the world than any other photographic medium," says George Rinhart of the Rinhart Galleries in New York. Fortunately thousands of these cards remain. In 1858, for instance, the London Stereoscopic Company advertised thousands of different photographs for sale, usually of architectural and topographic subjects. A year later the Stoddard Company in New York went into business, and many of their images were of western scenes by photographers recognized today for their superior skills.

(3) Daguerreotypes. One of the earliest forms of photography, a daguerreotype is an image on a silver-coated copper plate—usually a portrait. Since Daguerre wasn't able to master the duplicating process, no two daguerreotypes are alike. The result is a true collector's item, with prices inching higher all the time. Still, the word hasn't quite reached the boondocks. Last spring a country auction in Virginia netted one collector two dozen daguerreotypes for eighteen dollars—a real giveaway by New York standards.

(4) Tintypes, or ferrotypes. Like daguerreotypes, tintypes were mostly pictures of people. Taken on lacquered iron, they were less expensive than the

photos made on glass plates, the method that became the most common form of photography for many years. Snubbed by collectors for a while, tintypes are now coming into their own.

(5) *Cartes-de-visite.* Meant as a replacement for calling cards, *cartes-de-visite* sold by the hundreds of millions in the 1860's and 1870's in America and in Europe. Of royalty, politicians, writers, members of high society, music hall stars, courtesans, the photos are normally about 2¼ by 3½ inches, sepia toned, and mounted on cards. On the reverse side of the card or beneath the picture are printed the photographer's name and address, and frequently the name of the sitter too.

Other photographic images that are becoming more popular among collectors are travel pictures, usually of one hundred or so years ago. The Bisson brothers, Louis Auguste, and Auguste Rosalie excelled in this school in the early 1860's. The Bisson brothers took some of the most striking Alpine photographs in the history of the medium, and they indulged their love for beauty with images of French and Italian churches and cathedrals.

An exhibition last year at Asia House, in New York, of pictures taken in India by English and native photographers during the second half of the nineteenth century and early twentieth century has awakened collectors to photographs from that part of the world. Another extraordinary exhibition last year of photographs taken in Brazil from 1840 to 1920 turned New Yorkers' heads south of the border. Totally unknown outside of Brazil until their appearance at the Center for Inter-

Stereograms once provided popular and cheap entertainment and can still be found for as little as five dollars. Here, a man on Lookout Mountain, Tennessee.

Mount Williamson—Clearing Storm, *Ansel Adams: an acknowledged masterpiece by a great American landscape photographer*

Satiric Dancer, *André Kertész: a rare document of times past by a famous internationalist*

American Relations, on Park Avenue, the pictures are "of equivalent quality and variety to the work being done during the same period anywhere else in the world," according to Weston Naef, guest curator of the show.

Other fields that have been demanding more attention recently are fashion photography and the pre–World War II Hollywood photos. A show at Knoedler's in New York in April, 1976, that included Cecil Beaton's full-length portrait of Gary Cooper, his photo of Tallulah Bankhead, Eisenstaedt's Will Rogers, and Horst's Joan Crawford helped fan the flames of collectors' desire for the nostalgic, beautifully composed Hollywood prints. At the same time, early fashion photographs by Baron de Meyer, Edward Steichen, Peter Rose Pulham, Louise Dahl-Wolfe, George Hoyningen-Huene, and, again, Horst are all stepping outside their labels of commercial photography and becoming collectible.

In fact, collecting so-called commercial photography, which began seriously only about two years ago, is anticipated to be one of the most exciting areas of future collecting. Long neglected by dealers and collectors because it is done for advertising and editorial use, commercial photographers' work is now being looked at with a fresh eye. It

should not be forgotten that Steichen worked for the J. Walter Thompson Agency and that his compositions for Jergens lotion and Eastman Kodak were proclaimed as milestones of photography at the time.

While the work of such masters as Irving Penn, who has included advertising work in his repertoire, can now be purchased through a gallery, more often than not collectors must still seek out commercial photographers' works directly from their creators. "I have had requests for years from the public for my work," says Pete Turner, "and I confess I haven't paid much attention to them. Now, though, with the spotlight turned more in our direction, even more collectors are asking me to print them an image. I can see that I will have to do something about it . . . soon." Hiro, a Richard Avedon pupil, is another artist whose genius behind a camera is sought after, but whose prints are hard to obtain.

Deborah Turbeville, a former staff member of *Mademoiselle* magazine, is now a photographer whose dreamlike scenes are already cashing in on the demand by collectors for fashion's outré look. Printing limited-edition black-and-white images at three hundred dollars apiece, Turbeville's creations are described by *Newsweek* as "choreo-

graphed like ballet . . . they look like scenes out of Bertolucci or Antonioni's alienated *The Red Desert*."

Then there is Helmut Newton, a star of French *Vogue*. In his book *White Women*, Newton shocks by showing women with one breast protruding, or who crack whips and strike erotic poses in black garter belts and boots—inevitably with flagrant overtones of lesbianism. And Guy Bourdin, one of the most daring fashion photographers in Paris, brought his subcult creativity to Bloomingdale's department store in Manhattan recently. He picked out six girls whose looks he liked and posed them in various stages of lacy undress for the pages of the store's color catalogue. The promotion piece has all the potential of becoming a document worthy of collection.

"Bourdin is one of my favorite photographers," says Duane Michals, whose dream photographs are among the most collectible images on the market. "And I love fashion photography. I shoot a lot of it myself. But I don't consider fashion photographs as 'art.' They're interesting sociologically, historically, but they are exactly what they depict. They reflect what is in vogue at the moment they were shot. They don't, therefore, have the mark of infinity. They aren't what the photographer *wants* to photograph. They are what he's been paid to shoot. If a collector is willing to accept these parameters, fine. But he should be aware that like so much in life, a great deal depends on the definitions."

Consider, for instance, press photography. Is it collectible? Some people think so, including Cecil Beaton and Gail Buckland, authors of *The Magic Image*. "The public is too apt to take for granted the excellence of the photographs seen every day in the newspapers," they write. "It does not realize the expertise needed to capture the publishable picture. It does not realize that most probably [the photo] was taken under conditions of extreme difficulty, possibly even danger." Press photographs such as that of Queen Mary with the young Elizabeth and the Queen Mother at the funeral of King George VI, and Huynh Cong Ut's shattering picture of Vietnamese children fleeing from a fire bomb have registered indelibly in the minds of millions of viewers.

And so have many of the photographs of Arthur Fellig of New York, better known as "Weegee." Working at the start of his career as a printer in a news-picture agency in order to afford the film that he shot on his own time at night, the cigar-chewing, raucous, vainglorious Austrian immigrant stamped "Credit Weegee the Famous" on the back of his photographs. With a short-wave set by his bed, in which he slept with his clothes on, he was alerted to the city's disasters and was able to record them on film, frequently before the police arrived. Fires, crimes, accidents: they all intrigued Weegee. And the humorous did, too. One of his best-known photographs, taken in a nightclub, shows a tuxedoed drunk stroking a pig.

The work of many of the early photojournalists is not owned by them but by the publications for which they worked. For instance, Margaret Bourke-White made many of her photos when she was on the staff of *Fortune*; their sale through a gallery produces revenue for Time-Life as well as for the gallery itself. "It never occurred to the

Male Singers of the Metropolitan House in Last-Minute Rehearsal for Opening Night, *Weegee: a news photo grown into a classic*

photographer or his employer in many cases that these people's work would eventually be thought of as collectible," says Cusie Pfeifer of the Marcuse Pfeifer Gallery in Manhattan. "Nowadays, however, a photojournalist or any other photographer hired to do special assignments for publishers or companies tries to make sure that his contract reads that he maintains the rights to his work."

All photographers, in fact, are wising up to the larger market for their work. But many collectors find it too time consuming to track down the photographers whose work they admire in the media. But Howard Daitz, a private dealer, has gone to great lengths to get what he wants. "I would see a reproduction in magazines that I liked," he says, "and would take as much as six months to track down the photographer. I would write him for a print, and then maybe a year later I would get it."

Dance photography also fascinates collectors. Barbara Morgan, a pioneer in the field, spent five years recording the movements of Martha Graham. Emil Otto Hoppé's studies of the Diaghilev ballet corps are highly valued, and Richard Avedon's strobe shots of Rudolf Nureyev also attract certain collectors.

So do photographs, both old and new, that are printed on cloth, leather, enamel, porcelain, and artificial ivory. Another special area of collecting is historical photographs that deal with one subject: the construction of the Empire State Building, life in Harlem in the 1920's and 1930's, antique motorcars, suffragettes, the laying of the tracks of the transcontinental railroad.

Specialization of one kind or another will be the name of the game in future photography collecting, the dealers and many collectors themselves predict. The rising prices for rare prints will make broad-based collections of first-quality images harder to afford. Even if one's funds are unlimited, the supply is not. Collectors of photographs will do what collectors in other fields have done—concentrate in one area or one school—and be more challenged in the process. As there are collectors of Georgian silver, Louis XIV furniture, or American primitive paintings, so there will soon be specialists who collect only fashion photography of the thirties, or nineteenth-century portraits, or work by the leading living photographers. □

Landt and Lisl Dennis are husband and wife and a writer/photographer team. This article is adapted from their book Collecting Photographs: A Guide to the New Art Boom, *published this month by E. P. Dutton.*

FUTURE SUBJUNCTIVE

Girl with an Incredible Feeling

Accompanied by a stiff marching beat, a chorus of young actors sprays the stage with saliva as it sings the lines of a didactic Turkish poet: "We take life seriously by not thinking about it,/Without looking for something above or beyond." But even though they seem to threaten the audience with this creed, one by one a child's grin overtakes each face, until the whole group is laughing and shouting.

This is the cast of *Nightclub Cantata*, a cabaret revue written and directed by Elizabeth Swados, who also appears onstage as one of those serious children. Only twenty-five, and still looking like the Bennington College folk singer she was, Miss Swados (second cousin of the late novelist Harvey Swados) has quickly gained recognition as one of the most innovative composers in the contemporary musical theatre.

Already behind her are musical scores for a Greek trilogy directed by Andrei Serban and for Bertolt Brecht's *Good Woman of Setzuan*. She used to perform regularly with Pete Seeger, has worked in Africa with British director Peter Brook, was the subject of a documentary film, and has recently written and illustrated a children's book called *The Girl with the Incredible Feeling*. Now two of Joseph Papp's productions in New York, *The Cherry Orchard* and *Agamemnon*, feature her music.

She is the first to call these successes transitory, which is why she is still able to put together and perform new works of her own. *Nightclub Cantata*, performed in a Greenwich Village theatre in Manhattan, is an energetic collection of poetry, memory, and farce, all set to nonstop music. Jazz scats, Hebraic folk songs, Indian raga, calypsos, ballads, blues, and even fifties' shuffles all

CARRIE BORETZ

Composer Swados at a rehearsal of The Cherry Orchard *in New York*

weave through the show as part of a single composition.

Speaking of the lyrical diversity of her music, she says, "I have to be humble if I'm going to preserve someone else's words, but also very, very arrogant to pretend their words are actually mine." So her troupe sings verses by Pablo Neruda, Muriel Rukeyser, Sylvia Plath, Delmore Schwartz, and Elizabeth Swados —and the audience still feels as if one very personal voice is being heard. Some of the words are growled and cawed and cackled, while some are echoed perfectly by two competing voices. There are monologues, dialogues, and occasionally diatribes—but they are all part of Miss Swados's celebration of language. This naive wish to communicate with everything and everybody is what

really makes her music so special. For it takes a serious child indeed to demand, as she does in one of her songs: "I want to know this world!"

Yes!

Robert Wilson, the man who won a measure of acclaim last fall when his four-and-a-half hour *Einstein on the Beach* was presented on the stage of the Metropolitan Opera in New York, has a problem. His plays (or "operas," as he calls them by way of acknowledging their epic grandeur) are dreamlike and plotless. To allay the anxiety of audiences in search of a subject, he usually names his works after famous men. Besides *Einstein*, he has staged *The Life and Times of Sigmund Freud* and *The Life and Times of Joseph Stalin*, neither of

which made much reference to its title character.

Contemplating his next work, Wilson has come up with a new stratagem. He would put all the "plot" into the title. His first inspiration was *I Was Sitting on My Patio, This Guy Appeared, I Thought I Was Hallucinating*. But, on reconsideration, he thought of an even more informative name—one that tells all one needs to know about a Wilson plot—*No!*

A Loaf of Bread, a Glass of Wine, and Hushpuppies

The Spoleto Festival, that major cultural bash and Italian summer holiday, will present its first American season from May 25 to June 5 in Charleston, South Carolina, thus finally fulfilling the original vision of its founder, Gian Carlo Menotti, who years ago subtitled the event "Festival of Two Worlds."

Menotti himself spans the two cultures: born in Italy, he has spent most of his professional life as a composer in America, and his two Pulitzer Prize–winning operas, *The Medium* (1946) and *The Saint of Bleecker Street* (1954), ran successfully on Broadway before touring Europe. Menotti created the Spoleto Festival twenty years ago as "a popular feast in which the artist . . . could nourish the community at large—a place where art could be a loaf of bread and not a petit four." It claims to be the world's most comprehensive arts festival, a three-week offering of hearty fare, and indeed there will be all kinds of art at Charleston—performing and visual, classical and avant-garde —produced by established masters and youthful experimenters.

Some works that were highlights of former seasons at Spoleto will be featured, among them Tchaikovsky's opera *The Queen of Spades* and Menotti's own *The Consul*. Menotti is also composing a new piece for brass quintet to open the festival, and the Eliot Feld Ballet Company will perform works first seen in New York last March. There will be operas by Bizet and Offenbach, and a new Simon Gray play directed by Stephen Hollis. Many events and exhibits will be held in parks and at historic churches and theatres, which abound in the charming eighteenth-century city.

Liberty for Sale

Want to buy the Statue of Liberty? All you need is $20,000 and a large living room, for this Liberty is a reconstruction by the irrepressible Red Grooms and his Ruckus Construction Company, and it is currently in storage awaiting a buyer—along with Ruckus versions of the Brooklyn Bridge (priced at about $80,000), Wall Street ($60,000), Chinatown ($20,000), and Chase Manhattan Bank ($16,000).

Also available are the Fulton Fish Market, the Stock Exchange, the World Trade Center, City Hall, Trinity Church, Forty-second Street, and Rockefeller Center. Interested collec-

Ruckus Statue of Liberty

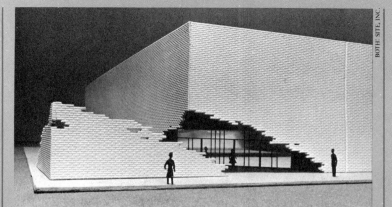

Design for Best Products: a "door" of ragged bricks

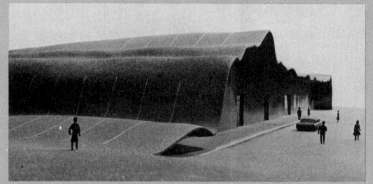

Another Site concoction: a show room covered by an undulating parking lot

tors should apply at the Marlborough Gallery in New York, where Grooms's zany celebration of Manhattan was exhibited last year.

Perhaps a well-heeled benefactor will buy all the pieces and provide them with permanent display space. In the meantime, Grooms's fans can make do with a new book about Ruckus Manhattan (published by George Braziller) for a mere $17.50 (hard cover) or $8.95 (paperback).

Tale of Two Capitals

Is Paris dead? "Practically," says Hilton Kramer, art critic for the *New York Times*. "The fact is," he wrote after attending the opening of the Pompidou Center, "the contemporary art scene in Paris is extremely dreary just now. When a visitor asks, 'Who are the most important artists now working in Paris?', the question leads to embarrassment, silence, and explanations, but very few names and no enthusiasm."

Will New York supersede London as the center of world traffic in works of art? There's no doubt about it, says Peter Wilson, chairman of Sotheby Parke Bernet and himself a Briton. It has nothing to do with economic hardship in

Britain. "It seemed that the British stopped buying before World War I," Wilson says, "when they were still immensely rich."

A Disaster Site

Modern American architecture has never been known for its sense of humor, but a whimsical New York firm named Site (originally an acronym for Sculpture in the Environment) aims to stir up its share of laughter. Its latest jokes are two show rooms in California for Best Products Company, a national mail-order firm whose Richmond and Houston show rooms it also designed.

Recently completed in Sacramento is a building that when seen at night is a windowless, doorless structure from which one corner seems to be cracking off. In the morning, an underground system of concealed motors and rails trolleys this triangular corner some twenty feet away to reveal a glass and chrome entrance to the building.

Site's upcoming *jeu d'esprit*, planned for 1978, is a parking lot that will completely conceal a Best show room in southern California. "When constructed," a Site brochure announces, "the show room will appear as though buried under a casual

series of massive undulations in the paving."

Site's byword is "de-architecturalization," a tongue twister that means a dedication to demolition, deterioration, deformation—or, as James Wines, the founder of Site, puts it, the condition of "reversing and removing some quality or element from architecture." The Best show room in Houston illustrates the principle: the façade is just an uneven, flat wall, except that an avalanche of bricks is pouring down on the pedestrian canopy.

Site's satirical itch has not won it any affection from the architectural establishment; in fact, the leading architectural journals have, until recently, refused to take the firm's activities seriously. But there are consolations. The recently opened Pompidou Center in Paris is planning an exhibition of Site's work for 1978. And Best Products reports a 50 per cent increase in business at its Houston center.

Cry, Clown, Cry?

It's getting so that moviegoers are finding it ever more difficult to know how to react to what's up there on the screen. Even in such a sophisticated picture as Alain Resnais's *Providence*, audiences

Joan Blondell, film star in the dark

laugh at scenes that were patently designed to enlist their sympathy. Or they wonder whether it's all just a gigantic, ambiguous put-on. But more confusion is on the way. Listen to Joan Blondell as she was filming John Cassavetes's free-swinging *Opening Night*, in which characters improvise their dialogue. "Don't ask me whether it's supposed to be a comedy or a drama," she moaned. "I'll have to see it before I can tell."

GUERNICA:
An Act of War, a Work of Art

By CHARLES L. MEE, JR.

Forty years ago this month, on May 1, 1937, Pablo Picasso picked up a pencil in his Paris studio and on a small rectangle of blue paper sketched a rough composition of a horse, a bull with a bird on its back, and a woman holding a lamp.

This drawing was the start of what was eventually to become the most renowned painting by the century's most protean artist. It was Picasso's response, in a spasm of controlled fury, to the bombing of the Basque village of Guernica five days earlier by Ger-

man pilots in the Spanish civil war.

The attack on Guernica was not the first against civilians in the history of warfare or even the first by twentieth-century bombers. And it was ultimately surpassed in horror by round-the-clock devastation of English and German cities. But because it was taken up by Picasso and transformed by him into an astonishing fusion of history and art, it has become a soaring monument of public and private anguish, a universal symbol of the crime of war against innocents.

Guernica burning in the wake of the bombing, April 26, 1937

Picasso's first sketch for the painting, with the bull, left; the horse, upended, center; and the woman, top

The artist in the Paris studio where he painted Guernica

General Francisco Franco, commander in chief of the nationalist forces, leaves rebel headquarters in Burgos, Spain, early in 1937.

Guernica is a village in the farm country of northern Spain, a few miles south of the coast of the Bay of Biscay and not far from the town of Bilbao. Guernica, settled in a broad valley among hills and orchards and farmlands, looks like any one of the neighboring farm towns: it has its plane trees, a market square, where stalls are set out on Mondays, several churches and convents, a public school in whose courtyard dances are held, shops and bakeries, a large plaza in front of the railroad station, and a sturdy old bridge of metal, stone, and concrete—the Rentería bridge.

But Guernica stands apart from its neighbors, and has stood apart for centuries, as the ancient capital of the Basques, a fiercely independent, democratic people. Before the time of written records, the elected leaders of the Basques were required to take an oath in front of a great sacred oak tree at the center of Guernica to respect the rights of the people. By the sixteenth century, when the Basques were finally absorbed into Castile and ruled by the Spanish monarchy, the king still respected the tradition and sent a representative, or went himself, to swear by the oak to observe the *fueros*, the separate and democratic rights of the Basques.

During the Spanish civil war of the 1930's, the Basques sided with the Republican gov-

ernment against the military rebellion led by General Francisco Franco and aided by troops sent by Hitler and Mussolini. The Republicans attracted the support of the Spanish democrats, but their cause became, too, an international cause. "Just like any honest man," Ernest Hemingway said, "I am against Franco and fascism in Spain." The Republicans soon found that they were championed by all manner of democrats, socialists, and Communists—even halfheartedly by the Soviet government (so halfheartedly, some maintain, as to have been intentionally harmful)—as well as by George Orwell, George Bernard Shaw, and Arthur Koestler.

Guernica, then, has been the home of ancient Basque liberties and an inspirer, too, of more modern democrats. "Guernica," said Jean Jacques Rousseau in the eighteenth century, "has the happiest people in the world, regulating their affairs by a body of peasants under an oak, and always conducting themselves wisely."

On April 26, 1937, a Monday, a clear, quiet, sunny market day, when the square by the Calle Fernando el Catolico and Calle del Senorio de Vizcaya was filled with farmers and sheep, horses and ox carts, and women doing their shopping, and the plaza in front of the railroad station was filled with people waiting for a train and children out playing,

at about four-thirty in the afternoon First Lieutenant Rudolf von Moreau of the German Condor legion, flying a Heinkel-111, eased gently down to four thousand feet and came neatly in over the center of town at about 150 miles an hour with a three-thousand-pound load of bombs—high explosives, antipersonnel shrapnel, and incendiary bombs.

According to *Guernica: The Crucible of World War II*, the meticulous report recently put together by Gordon Thomas and Max Morgan Witts, a bartender named Juan Silliaco saw the first bombs fall near the railroad station. He saw a "group of women and children. They were lifted high into the air, maybe twenty feet or so, and they started to break up. Legs, arms, heads, and bits and pieces flying everywhere."

Silliaco, his own arms and legs lacerated, stumbled over the lower half of a woman as he set out to help the wounded. The loudest screams, he noticed, "came from a group of women tearing at the pile of rubble in front of the Julián Hotel." The hotel's façade had fallen where a group of small children had been playing. Inside one bomb crater near the railway station lay the decapitated body of Juliana Oleaga, recognizable from her dress, and the body of twelve-year-old Florence Madariaga, recognizable "by the pigtail attached to what remained of her scalp."

90

Picasso's hatred of the rightist cause led him, even before the bombing of Guernica, to produce two sheets of small etchings (one is above), which he called Dream and Lie of Franco.

The first bomber finished its run, and a lull of twenty minutes or so followed.

• • •

At the time of the bombing of Guernica Pablo Picasso was in Paris—in a large studio he had fitted up in a seventeenth-century house on the Left Bank. He had been commissioned several months before—in January, 1937—by the Republican government of Spain to paint a mural for the Spanish pavilion at the Paris World's Fair, scheduled to open in May. The mural was meant to be a work that would attract attention and support for the Spanish republic, whose cause Picasso had championed from the very first. But Picasso could think of no suitable subjects for a work so important to him. Earlier in the year, he had produced a set of etchings called *Dream and Lie of Franco*, accompanied by his own poem of rage: ". . . cries of children cries of women cries of birds cries of flowers cries of timbers and of stones cries of bricks cries of furniture of beds of chairs of curtains of pots of cats and of papers cries of odors which claw at one another cries of smoke pricking the shoulder of the cries which stew in the caldron and of the rain of birds which inundates the sea which gnaws the bone and breaks its teeth biting the cotton wool which the sun mops up from the plate which the purse and the pocket hide in the print which the foot leaves in the rock."

In the last several days of April and the first few days of May, the Paris newspapers began to carry reports of the bombing of Guernica. "Milles bombes incendiaires," reported the Communist *L'Humanité*, "lancées par les avions de Hitler et [*L'Humanité* erred] de Mussolini réduisent en cendres la ville de Guernica." *Le Figaro* carried a photograph of the smashed buildings and the smoking, rubble-strewn streets; and *L'Humanité* ran a peculiarly haunting picture of a dead woman lying on her back, remarkably peaceful, her dark hair damp, it seemed, from the blood that flowed from her crushed skull. Her hair suggested the shape of the helmet of an old Roman hero.

"In the form of its execution," George L. Steer cabled to the *New York Times*, "and the scale of the destruction it wrought . . . the raid on Guernica is unparalleled in military history. Guernica was not a military objective. A factory producing war material that lay outside the town was untouched."

Other horrible events had occurred in wars before this; Sherman's march through Georgia had not spared civilians; Tamerlane was not a gentle warrior; the Crusades were brutal. But henceforth it appeared that no one and nothing—not farmers at market or bakers in their shops, not women or children or homes or schools or convents or churches or oxen or horses or birds—were safe from bombs falling, without warning, from the air.

Peter Green, canon of Manchester, St. Philip's Clergy House in Salford, England, wrote a letter on April 29 to the Manchester *Guardian*. "The object of modern war," he said, "is not to defeat or even to destroy armies in the field. The object of modern war is so to demoralize the civil population as to break the nation's will to war and put an end to war-resistance. . . . There is no end to modern war except the utter collapse of modern civilisation. . . . Either civilisation must put an end to war or war will put an end to civilisation."

• • •

On May 1 Picasso made a pencil sketch on a small piece of light blue paper. On the left is a bull with a bird sitting on its back. At the center is a horse—apparently on its back, seemingly dead, with its hoofs raised in the air. To the right a woman leans out of an open window on what may be the second floor of a building. At the extreme right is another squiggle—perhaps a wall or a stick figure. Along the bottom of the drawing are more scribbles—perhaps a mass of bodies.

Later that same day, on another piece of the same light blue paper, Picasso made two more sketches. On the top half of this piece of paper he turned the bull around to face the woman holding the lantern. On the bottom half he moved the bull again, this time into

MME PICASSO, *1923*

NUDE WOMAN IN A RED ARMCHAIR, *1932*

Picasso's personal life was in turmoil at the time he painted Guernica: *he was separated from his wife, Olga, top; he had frequent quarrels with his mistress, Marie-Thérèse Walter, the model for the painting above; and he was living—at least part of the time—with a painter and photographer, Dora Maar, below.*

PORTRAIT OF DORA MAAR, *1937*

the foreground, and turned it around again, facing left. He moved the horse to the extreme left; it is alive now, right side up, with its head and neck reaching upward in a shriek of pain. And on the bull's back is not a bird but a tiny winged horse, the Pegasus of Greek myth, which helped the hero Bellerophon to defeat the monster Chimera.

Still later that same day, Picasso filled a piece of paper with horses in different attitudes—neck extended, phalluslike, upward; neck bent in agony, its side pierced by a horrible wound. On yet another piece of paper, he drew a simple outline of a horse, as though he was merely reminding himself to think about horses. Then, on a fifth piece of paper, he drew a horse collapsing in pain and terror, its legs sketched in several different attitudes as the animal appears to sink to the ground.

Finally, in his last sketch of the day, is another attempt to outline the whole composition: the bull is again to the left, facing away from the center of the scene; the horse (with a Pegasus emerging from the wound in its side) collapses in the center foreground, extending its neck in a hopeless effort to rise; the woman to the right holds her lamp out from the window to the center of the drawing; and at the bottom right lies a soldier—dead, holding a spear, peaceful, wearing what appears to be the helmet of an old Roman hero.

This composition is full of confusion: the very center is much too full of the hindquarters of the bull; the lower left corner is a tangle of assorted feet and the horse's hindquarters; the woman holding the lamp looks removed and useless; and the miniature Pegasus looks silly. Yet here, at the end of his first day's work, is the basis of Picasso's *Guernica*, which he was to finish, in a paroxysm of work, in about six weeks.

The most astonishing aspect of Picasso's first day of work on *Guernica* is surely its savage coolness. He does not show bloody bits and pieces of women and children flying through the air; he does not show smashed buildings; he does not depict massive death by fire; the woman with the lamp who leans out of the window is not horrified but rather curious; and the dead soldier lies at peace.

Whatever violent emotions Picasso may have felt have been thoroughly subdued. He does not try to depict the bombing of Guernica, to illustrate it, or even quite to make it into an allegory. Rather, he brings the event deeply within himself, and he responds to it as a unique witness. His first reaction is

transmuted, strangely, into the silently whinnying anguish of the horse—a horse that has been injured by the bombing of Guernica, obviously, but more than that; it is a symbolic horse of some sort, a vexingly obscure, seemingly irrelevant, private symbol of some sort, a peculiar association of the sort that springs unbidden to the mind.

"The horse," said Picasso's friend Juan Larrea emphatically, "generally represents a woman who played an exceptionally important part in [Picasso's] life." It is a bizarre thought—that the center of this painting, in response to a terrible public event, should be so private, even erotic. Yet it is the ancient and optimistic response, to greet death with the life force, Thanatos with insistent Eros.

Picasso was just then emerging from some of the most painful emotional conflicts of his life, from a separation from his wife, Olga, and from a tumultuous time with his mistress, Marie-Thérèse Walter, who had already given birth to his daughter and whom he was prevented from marrying by maddening legal complications. And when he painted *Guernica* he was involved with yet another woman, Dora Maar. During all this time, between 1933 and 1937, he had been preoccupied with drawings and etchings of bullfights, of bulls and horses, and of a Minotaur and a woman—pictures that sometimes depict gentle affection, sometimes fierce passion, sometimes violence, hatred, rape, murder. A woman writhes in bed, as though she had been stabbed, or gored by a bull. A bloodthirsty bull lays bare a horse's innards, or explores the horse's wounded side with erotic intensity. At times the bull and horse are combined with a female torero; at times the bull carries off the torero, the Minotaur mounts the woman; and, in a late drawing, the Minotaur removes his mask to reveal a gentle, bearded man, at ease with a woman and child. These were the obscure, private passions Picasso brought with him to a consideration of Guernica, and if the symbols are confusing, it is because they are confused, as his feelings were, as the terrible event that he considered was. The horse meant one thing and then another, then both, and then neither—and at last, perhaps, it contained just enough of all the associations that had occurred to Picasso to be left alone. It suggested the event, it suggested an allegory, and it recalled to Picasso his most private feelings; and so it served. Indeed, it is exactly this fusion of his most personal fantasies with the public event that gives his painting its power, just as with most of us it is the personal associations we have with public events that cause them to impress themselves deeply on our feelings and on our memories.

. . .

This horse will not stand still. It is a woman. It is Picasso's estranged wife; it is his mistress. Then again the horse, Juan Larrea said on another occasion, represents Republican Spain. And the horse, as Picasso told a young American who sought out the great man for a free-lance newspaper interview, represents "the people."

If the horse will not stay put, what of the bull? The bull, Picasso told his American friend, represents brutality.

Fascism?

"No," said Picasso, "the bull is not fascism, but it is brutality and darkness."

Yet the bull does not look brutal or villainous. The bull may have just gored the horse, but perhaps it has not. In the bullfight the bull is the victim, not the horse. Yet here the bull does not seem to be the victim. Perhaps, symbol of brutality that it is, it is also a symbol of strength and virility, reminiscent of ancient Mediterranean incarnations of divinity.

The symbolism of *Guernica* shifts, suggesting now this, now that. We never lose the essential message—that an awful deed has been perpetrated—but the symbols disintegrate and merge and are chaotic at times, as war is, as the aftermath of a bombing is, holding many meanings, many hidden threats, many tormenting and tragic mysteries connected with chance death and awful design. Only the little winged Pegasus had a clear, symbolic meaning derived from classical mythology, and after this first day of sketching, the Pegasus disappeared from Picasso's studies and never found its way back into the final painting.

To those who kept asking him whether the bull meant this, the horse that, Picasso finally answered (desperately) in a letter to the director of New York's Museum of Modern Art: "But, this bull is a bull, this horse is a horse. There is also a sort of bird, a chicken or a pigeon, I no longer remember, on the table. This chicken is a chicken. Of course, the symbols . . . but it is not necessary that the painter create them, these symbols. . . . It is necessary that the public, the spectators, see in the horse, in the bull, symbols that they interpret as they understand them. There are animals: these are massacred animals. That is all, for me; let the public see what it wants to see."

STUDY FOR THE HORSE, *May 1*

MOTHER WITH DEAD CHILD, *May 9*

BULL WITH HUMAN FACE, *May 11*

For weeks Picasso drew and redrew the basic elements of his composition, exploring different styles and combining human and animal forms.

Von Moreau joined a wave of bombers at Garay, about ten miles south of Guernica, and led them, along with six Messerschmitt BF-109's, up north to Elanchove on the coast, then back around on a southwesterly course for the bombing run over Guernica. According to Thomas and Witts, "A cluster of incendiaries landed among the fifty girls tending vats and molds in the candy factory.

The bombs exploded with white flashes, then flared and burned fiercely, scattering red-and-white fragments of Thermit. [The] factory manager . . . emerged from his office in time to see a cascade of sparks envelop one of the girls, setting her overalls and hair alight. She collapsed in a fiery ball.

"An incendiary landed in a bull pen, spraying two bullocks with burning Thermit.

93

Maddened with pain, they broke out of the stall and charged through the market before falling into a bomb crater. Smoke killed caged birds."

The fire station "disappeared in smoke." Its destruction was so sudden and so complete that "it would be three days before the stable boy's body was recovered, intermingled with the remains of two dray horses."

That the fire station was destroyed was of no importance anyway. The commercial center of Guernica was composed principally of old wood-frame buildings, and the narrow streets made fine wind tunnels to fan the flames. Almost three-quarters of the town would be destroyed by fire. Guernica burned at full blast, leaving behind the keen scent of burnt plaster, wood, and flesh.

Some people managed to get to shelters. "A row of bombs fell along the street," Antonio Arazamagni recalled. "One after another, in a line, like a pack of cards, the houses began to collapse. . . . The shelter went, too. All the explosions fused together. The force of the blast threw three people out of the shelter."

A Heinkel-51 flew along a narrow street at the center of town, and its pilot machine-gunned Jacinta Gómez. Her three children ran from the house out to their mother. A second Heinkel-51 buzzed the street and cut them down. Now hundreds of men and women and children were "running in all directions through the town, aimlessly."

. . .

During the next ten days, Picasso worked through another dozen and a half sketches. He struggled with the horse's head, the viselike teeth, the swordlike tongue (suggesting "piercing cries"). In one sketch he tried to put the horse's upper teeth outside its mouth, as though growing out of its nose. The old cubist and surrealist devices were particularly suited to suggesting that war violates nature itself, that war breeds monstrosities and produces genetic mutants. In a drawing of May 10, the horse has collapsed and tries to get up. Its chest and head are on the ground, one foreleg is bent under its neck, the other foreleg is extended, trying to push up. In another drawing, the horse's eyes are shown both frontally and in profile; one nostril is turned sideways, producing a sense of squeezing, twisting, compression.

The bull runs away, is uninvolved, or wishes to appear innocent. Then again the bull is alert, and then in another sketch its eyes look threatening, or stare, astonished, paralyzed; it is attracted by the light, or

frightened by it; then, in yet another sketch, it appears noble, the incarnation of strength, beauty, and virtue. Then again it is ferocious, then imperturbable, then, at last, withdrawn from the very center of the composition, it stands aside, powerful, removed, watching, as the artist watches.

The dead soldier is transmogrified into a piece of sculpture, a broken statue, a shattered ideal, perhaps, from a vanquished tradition of chivalry, recalling that great early Renaissance painting of warfare, of whinnying horses and broken spears on the ground—Paolo Uccello's *Rout of San Romano*. A sketch for the statue's hand shows six fingers clutching the handle of the broken sword. More monsters of war.

A woman holds a dead baby. Her head is thrown back in anguish and terror. Her eyes are wide with hopeless horror. The child's head is thrown back, and farther back, and hangs lifelessly upside-down, its nostrils exposed grotesquely. The child emerges from the mother's body, covered with blood. The mother's breasts tumble, full and useless, over the dead child's body. The mother runs. The mother falls, descends a ladder from a burning house. Her head is thrown back until it is upside-down. Blood oozes between her fingers. The mother's eyes, shaped like tears, turn, twist, spin, are upside-down. Blood covers her breasts. She cries out, her tongue a sword. Her eyes stare, immobile; her eyes are unbelieving. Her eyes stare from two profiles at once, having too much belief and too little, and she cries out. Her eyes turn, her head turns, her nostrils turn, her tongue turns, her eyes have tears that cut arcs into her face, tears like sharp wires, eyes within eyes, frightened, falling, the child mute, blind, quiet, the mother's head and eyes and tears spinning, tongue thrust out.

Long after he finished painting *Guernica*, Picasso would go on drawing and painting this crying woman—through the summer and late into the autumn, apparently having to work himself back down from this moment of his painting. Dora Maar was living with him at the time, and Picasso painted her during the succeeding months in every attitude of anguish and despair—continuing to mix private and public agony in an ultimately unfathomable way.

. . .

Von Knauer, Von Beust, and Von Krafft led their air squadrons in over Guernica at 120 miles an hour. "I saw a man," Juan Silliaco recalled to Thomas and Witts, "crawling down the street, dragging his

broken legs. He was saying, 'Help me, please help me.' Then he just disappeared along with some cows which had broken free from their pens at the market. They were literally blown to pieces. Pieces of people and animals were lying everywhere. The bombs were falling all around and the ground was rocking beneath my feet."

"So the attack went ahead," Von Krafft remembered. "The incendiary bombs made a silver shower over the smoke above Guernica."

"Fear . . . is very important," said Freiherr von Richthofen, chief of staff of this bomber legion, later a field marshal and a member of Hitler's personal staff, and the man credited with perfecting the aerial blitzkrieg, "because it affects morale. Morale is more important than weapons in winning battles. Continuously repeated, concentrated air attacks have the most effect on the morale of the enemy."

María Ortuza was in the bomb shelter under the town hall when a 550-pounder hit the civic building. She believed "we were being buried alive. The roof came down on us, and then the town hall was hit twice more. Three floors fell on our shelter." She crawled for the door, pushing aside a hand, then she found that the hand had caught hold of her belt, and then she discovered that she was dragging a severed arm with her.

Juan Silliaco, by this time, was huddled in a broken viaduct. "Close by, in the wreckage, was a young woman. I could not take my eyes off her. Bones stuck through her dress. Her head had been twisted right around her neck. She lay, mouth open, her tongue hanging out. I vomited and lost consciousness."

. . .

On May 11 Picasso began work on the canvas itself, a piece of unbleached muslin more than twenty-five feet long and eleven feet high—so large, in fact, that it had to be tilted backward slightly against the studio wall. To paint the upper portions Picasso had to use a ladder and a long-handled brush. The painting would never have color; it would be black and white, like a documentary photograph, with hues of blue-gray emerging from the pigments, and the hatch work Picasso used for the horse's hair suggested both a myriad of tiny wounds and newsprint.

He worked quickly, so quickly that he allowed the paint to drip here and there, and once, when he changed the position of the bull's head, he did not take the time to paint

On loan from the artist to the Museum of Modern Art in New York (above) since 1939, Guernica *will be sent to Spain, according to Picasso's wish, when a genuine republic has been restored. With Franco dead, an election for Parliament imminent, and a new constitution likely, that day may be approaching.*

out entirely one of the animal's eyes, so that the bull has the shadow of a third eye with which to gaze at the carnage around him.

Dora Maar watched him work, and from time to time she took a photograph of the canvas, and so today we are able to see the work in various stages of completion. The woman with the lamp who leans out the window (the interested but powerless outside world? a Greek chorus? a symbol of new light? resurrection? compassion? the objective light of history? Marie-Thérèse?) remains constant throughout. Her lamp marks the top of an equilateral triangle—the precise geometrical form Picasso chose to try to contain the chaos.

In the first stage of the mural, Picasso has sketched in five women: the woman with the lamp; a dead woman on the ground, who will be entirely eliminated; the woman holding the dead child, who will occupy the far left of the canvas; a woman at lower right, who is running toward, or away from, disaster; and at far right a woman who is falling from the burning building and who is herself on fire,

presumably from an incendiary bomb. The fingers on her right hand number six.

The horse is still at the center of the composition; the animal's neck is bent around so far that its head is upside-down. The bull faces left, leaving its hindquarters awkwardly in the center of the composition.

Unless the bull is the villain of this scene, all the figures in *Guernica* seem to be the victims of an unseen and therefore chillingly impersonal enemy; all who are slaughtered are innocent. Indeed, Picasso has not acknowledged the presence of anyone in *Guernica* who could fight back, or of any men except the hero at the bottom of the canvas.

This hero, who seemed to have been transformed into a statue in one of Picasso's sketches, has been brought back to life in the first stage of the mural itself. In fact, his arm reaches up, in a direct, strong vertical line, up as far as the woman's lamp, and there raises a clenched fist, a fist that becomes, momentarily, the new, defiant center of the painting.

In the second stage of the mural, the fist has been severed from the soldier's body and

has acquired a life of its own. It is larger, stronger, and it clutches several ears of corn. This massive, angry fist is then surrounded by a flaming halo—the sun with rays of sunflower petals—which dominates the scene triumphantly.

Yet surely this is absurd, for the people of Guernica had not triumphed, and Picasso's wishful thinking begins to look merely ridiculous. In the third stage of the painting, Picasso has removed the sunflower and the fist and the arm. The soldier no longer faces valiantly upward; he has been crushed, and his face is turned to the ground. There is no sign of any hope whatever. Eventually the halo will be transformed into a cold electric light bulb, and we are forced to observe that this scene is neither outdoors nor indoors, but both; it is neither day nor night, but both; it is neither a private statement nor a public one, but both; it is neither a nightmare nor a vision, but both.

In the fourth stage, in the space where the arm and the fist had been, the horse's head is now raised in tortured, painful rage and des-

95

At the bottom of the canvas, almost exactly in the center, one small symbol of life, a flower, exists among all the images of horror.

peration. The hindquarters of the bull have been turned around again, into the upper left portion of the mural, but now its massive head is turned, with what seems to be enormous effort, back around to the left so that it can look backward and forward—and out at the spectator as well. If it seemed ambiguous before, the bull is now the very quintessence of ambiguity, facing both ways at once, looking in all directions, at once present and distant, dark and light, strong and compassionate, powerful and powerless. With its great torso turned around, it has become, too, a protective enclosure for the grieving mother and her dead child—the patriarch of a family group. All heads save that of the dead soldier and of the falling, burning woman turn to the bull, and he can do nothing. In the finished painting, astonishingly, the eyes of the bull resemble the eyes in one of Picasso's own self-portraits.

• • •

The biggest problem after the three-hour attack was over, said Augusto Unceta, "was matching up the bits and pieces of the bodies." Fires burned in Guernica through the night and were not finally brought under control until the middle of the next day. When the final accounting was completed, it was reckoned that the Condor legion had dropped one hundred thousand pounds of explosives on Guernica.

A spokesman for General Franco promptly disclaimed all responsibility for the bombing. That very night one of his generals said on the radio that it must have been the Basques themselves who blew up the town, so they could blame the atrocity on Franco. But in later years it was learned that Von Richthofen had conferred with Juan Vigón, his Spanish liaison and the chief of staff to General Emilio Mola, commander of Franco's army of the north; and word may have gone even further up the line of command. However, it does appear that Franco himself did not know that the Germans had bombed the sacred city of the Basques.

The German commanders of the Condor legion eventually admitted that they had attacked Guernica, saying that the town was a legitimate military target. They were trying, they said, to knock out an escape route for retreating Republican troops—the Rentería bridge, which was, in truth, a point of convergence of several routes of escape. Yet with this as their avowed purpose—and the rules of war would have permitted the bombers to hit the bridge if they had tried to avoid the town in doing so—they could not successfully explain why they had dropped incendiary bombs and antipersonnel shrapnel bombs to take out a metal and concrete bridge, nor why Freiherr von Richthofen had dispatched forty-three area bombers and strafing fighters instead of the precision Stuka dive bombers that he kept on the ground, nor why Von Richthofen, in his secret report to Berlin, had said the bombing of Guernica "was the greatest success," when the Rentería bridge, its avowed target, still stood after the attack, utterly untouched, as it stands even now.

The argument persists today, with new evidence put forward by one side and then the other. A new military target near Guernica is found—a munitions factory—and then it is learned that the Germans did not know of it at the time. And all the while, despite the repeated assertions of former Franco aides and German generals, no real evidence is found for the bizarre suggestion that the Basques destroyed their own town. And still the Rentería bridge stands.

Whether the bombing of the townspeople of Guernica was the result of conscious planning to induce fear in the enemy or only the result of an offhand contempt for civilian life and a casual interest in breaking enemy morale, the event has become a potent symbol. It has been considered a rehearsal for World War II and the beginning of a modern era of mass terror and the massacre of defenseless civilians in wartime—later in other parts of Spain, then at Lidice and Dresden, in Hiroshima and Nagasaki, and in Vietnam at My Lai.

Just how old or new such barbarousness may be is a moot point, and Picasso seems to have meditated on the question. The style of his painting is that of the twentieth century, yet superimposed on the triangular composition (itself a form as ancient as the pyramid) are the divisions of a medieval triptych: the panel at the left is the bull, at the center, the horse, and at the right, the falling, burning woman. Whether novel or ancient, whether done by bombs or spears, such an act, Picasso seems to say, can never be justified.

In his work on the final details of the painting, Picasso added a small bird on a table in the darkness behind the bull; he made even clearer the definition of a spear falling from above to pierce the horse; on the ground he drew in the lines of Spanish tiles, suggestive of a grid, and an arrow, recalling the neat target markers on military maps. At the bottom of the mural, in the center, he left undisturbed a small, barely perceptible flower, a timid expression of hope, somewhat sentimental, but an expression of hope nonetheless.

Before he was finished he murdered the warrior definitively, decapitated him, transformed him back into a broken statue, and turned him face up again, his eyes falling loosely over his face, and his mouth agape in a permanent, mute, horror-stricken cry. □

Charles L. Mee, Jr.'s most recent book, A Visit to Haldeman and Other States of Mind, *was published in March.*